The Art of Being Human

Deborah Ravetz

 Vala

First published in 2016 by Vala Publishing Co-operative

Copyright © Deborah Ravetz

Vala Publishing Co-operative Ltd
8 Gladstone Street, Bristol, BS3 3AY, UK

For further information on Vala publications, see
www.valapublishers.coop or write to info@valapublishers.coop

Cover artwork by Richard Heys

Typeset in Freya
Printed and bound by CPI Antony Rowe, Chippenham, UK
The paper used is Munken Premium, which is FSC certified.

A CIP catalogue record for this title is available from
the British Library.

ISBN 978-1-908363-15-2

For my mother and father who gave me life

For my husband and my friends
who gave me a harbour

About the Author

Deborah Ravetz was born in Zambia in 1957 and left Africa ten years later. Since then she has lived in both Britain and Germany. She has studied art, philosophy and literature as part of her quest to understand what it means to be human. She sees the whole realm of art and ideas in this light; they embody our attempt to live deeply.

She works as a lecturer specialising in Art and the Development of Consciousness, and also as a painter and a Social Sculpture practitioner. What this is will become clear after reading this book.

In her early thirties she became aware of how very few people love their work. Out of this she developed a method of helping people explore their lives and find their vocation.

Deborah is married and lives with her husband in East Sussex.

Contents

Contents

Foreword

If we want to make a difference in the world around us, and to do this without violence, then the only instrument we have is our selves. And so if we want to develop our capacity to make a difference, then we must develop ourselves.

This work of authentic self-development is necessary but also extraordinarily, even existentially challenging. Most of us therefore shy away from this work, preferring the lazier path of pretending that we are fine and that it is others who must develop themselves. This ordinary path is futile and worthless.

Deborah Ravetz's book is outstandingly valuable because she has not shied away from her own work. She has reflected profoundly, courageously, and patiently on her own experiences, both gross and subtle, and through this reflection has developed her self and her capacity to make a difference.

Deborah has given us a great gift by writing about her experience and reflections so thoughtfully and touchingly. Her text is so honest and lyrical that it cannot but inspire us. In this way her work enables ours, and thereby makes an important difference in the world.

Adam Kahane, director of Reos Partners and author of
Power and Love: A Theory and Practice of Social Change

Chapter 1
Finding the Form

Art may be helpful in that we the artists bear our distresses more passionately, [that we] give perhaps now and then a clearer meaning to, and develop for ourselves, a means of expressing the suffering in ourselves and its conquest more precisely and clearly.
Rainer Maria Rilke[1]

S
even years ago I created a project called *The Search for the Deep Self*. Normally when I make a piece of artwork, all I can see is how it needs improvement. This time, I found myself loving my work and believing in it unreservedly. I conceived this work during collaboration with several other artists. We had met while working on a presentation for an International Mask Festival: we were actors, dancers, visual artists and writers. Each of us had brought our expertise to the presentation. After our work was completed, we decided to get together for a conversation. We didn't know each other intimately, but the success of our first collaboration meant that we were eager to talk, and to explore the possibility of doing more work together. It was during this conversation that I found the form for my own life's work.

We were in my sitting room. The facilitator of our collaboration, and the director of the whole festival, was the actor and mask practitioner Mike Chase. He began the conversation by describing our mutual wish to free ourselves from what he described as a toxic culture of fame. He had realised that, instead of wasting his energy longing to be recognised by the mass media, he wanted to turn to his local community and to devise work in the community, for the community.

Mike had asked for help devising our presentation from a fellow actor, Katharine Messenger. Although a trained actor, she hadn't wanted to act in our piece. She was the one we all knew least but, despite helping us, she had remained distant. As she listened to Mike speak about his dream she became more and more animated and open. She connected deeply with what Mike was saying and she told us that she wanted to join him and help him to realise his project. She then told us the devastating story of her own career as an actor.

From the moment she had found out about the world of the theatre, she had known that was what she wanted to do. Her drama teacher had encouraged her. As soon as she could, she had gone to drama school and earned her Equity card. She imagined playing the great roles of classical theatre with intelligent and enlightened directors and thoughtful audiences. Theatre was her vocation, a spiritual calling. In reality her working life had proved to be a great disillusionment. She found herself working with people who treated the actors so appallingly that she was completely shattered. Broken-hearted, she left her work, her confidence in ruins. Very soon after, she met a much older man and moved in with him. She then went on to have three children and gave up all thought of the theatre.

She went on to tell us that, just before she had begun working with us, she had been rushed to hospital with a severe headache. The pain was so bad that she was convinced that she must have a life-threatening brain tumour. When the doctor examined her, he told her that her acute headaches were caused not by a tumour but by stress. Relieved, she had returned home, resolving to try and do something to mitigate her condition. Only when Mike began speaking had she finally discovered the cause of her stress. When her heart had been broken by her failed life in the theatre, she had decided that the only thing she could do to protect herself from future disappointment was to kill the actor in herself. She now realised that her terrible headache had been caused by the stress of trying to suppress her true identity. Listening to Mike, she connected with her inner actor, who was not only alive but also demanding to be given the space to unfold and flourish. There and then, she acknowledged the violence that she had done to her deepest core, and she resolved to put down her defences and dare to be vulnerable. Our group gave her hope that there might be a different way to be an actor, and she asked if she too could join us and reclaim that part of herself which had been buried for so long.

Katharine's story about her un-lived life echoed with my experiences, coming together in a potent mixture with my own concerns. At the time I was studying for a Masters degree in Social Sculpture, and I was preparing work for my final degree show. Social Sculpture widens the remit of art to include not only objects but also the stuff of our inner and social life as the medium for artistic creativity. I will talk about Social Sculpture in detail in Chapter 16.

I desperately wanted my work to grow out of something I really cared about, as well as reflect the essence and spirit of Social Sculpture. As I sat there, listening to Katharine and connecting with the different strands of inner and outer conversation, the image of my future project began to emerge. I saw in my mind's eye a room filled with banners, standing in a circle. On each of these banners would be a photograph of a person like Katharine. Underneath the photograph would be the story of their struggle for self-realisation.

I immediately asked Katharine to allow me to have her story.

She was bemused, as she had no sense of either having or telling a story. Up until then she had seen her life as a chaotic jumble of events. As I told her story back to her, the jumble became coherent. Not only did she see her story, she also saw the heroine of the story – she saw herself.

I then went on to ask my closest friends if they would allow me to include their stories in my room of banners. Like Katharine, they didn't see their own stories until I had retold what they had shared with me over many years. Generously, they all agreed and I began to collect and write accounts from all of them.

As the project grew, I also began to include the people whom I saw as my spiritual family. These are the people whom I knew from my own inner search, who had moved and inspired me at different times in my life. Some of them were long dead. Some were still alive. If they were still alive, I contacted them and asked them to allow me to include them in my work. As every person who became part of the project moved me in some way, the work grew organically out of my inner life.

When the banners were made, it was important to me that the people from my own life were placed alongside the world figures: side by side, as one community. I wanted to acknowledge that every moment of becoming is significant and deserves to be honoured, regardless of whether the person becomes well known or not. I made this project in 2007. I am constantly adding to my work as more and more people give me their stories. I feel the work will not be finished until it contains the story of every person in the world.

Katharine's story set my work in motion. She gave me a glimpse into her inner drama and helped me form my deepest question. This question is: if every person is a unique human being with infinite potential, what makes it so difficult for us to find that unique self and manifest that potential? Katharine had been frightened of being vulnerable. Her decision to try to protect herself from the pain of disappointment and failure had made her choose not to take the risk of trying to be who she really was. The details of her story were specific to her. Sadly however, the urge to protect ourselves in this way is something that many people can recognise in their own story. I saw that Katharine's attempt to rid herself of her longings was an attempt to exercise control over her life. She was afraid of life as process, life as constant movement and growth. I decided, there and then, that I would try to explore the whole territory of 'life as process' in order to discover why it makes us so fearful.

One of the people whom I regard as a member of my spiritual family is the German poet, Rainer Maria Rilke. In his poems *The Duino Elegies*[2] he explores the role of process and of transience, the role of struggle and of death. In the *Tenth Elegy* a recently dead young man is led first through the limited City of Pain, and then out into the wide reaches of the Land of Pain. The translators J B Leishman and Stephen Spender describe how Rilke reacted to this fear of the pain of process. They say:

> *Rilke collects and satirises, in the image or parable of the City of Pain, all that most repelled him in that half-hearted and half minded kind of life which had for so long been the object of his satire and astonishment – that half-life, from which death, and all that is mysterious and inexplicable, is simply excluded: that life whose consolations are provided by conventional religion, and whose activities are the pursuit of happiness and the making of money; from which fear and mystery are banished by distractions, and where suffering is regarded as an unfortunate accident. With this half-life, with this enclosed and limited City of Pain, he contrasts the spacious Land of Pain, which is Death, where the real meaning [the 'flowering'] of sadness is perceived, where, instead of a perpetual escape from reality through distractions, there is a perpetual progress in reality through painfully achieved insight, and where at last, the 'source of joy' is discovered.* [3]

Rilke was in touch with two ways of living life. One was intent on keeping the difficulties of life at bay. The other was prepared to embrace the whole of life. Rilke believed that reducing existence to nothing more than the pursuit of happiness and making money was a strategy to avoid facing the fact that there is much in life that we cannot control. Although we may seem to manage to suppress or deny life's complexity for a longer or shorter time, we will ultimately fail. We cannot tame life because all of us must die and no one can escape the fact that we all suffer. But Rilke gives us hope. He suggests that we can choose to embrace the whole of life, including the inexplicable and the difficult. Even more, he reassures us this will not destroy and overwhelm us as we fear. True, we may experience all the impact of our pain. We may also know long times of uncertainty and anxiety. However for him, these aspects of life are not mistakes; they have an important role in life, because they draw us below the surface to a deeper level of existence. When we endure our sadness, it can 'flower'. By bearing our pain we reach what he calls 'painfully achieved insights'. The pursuit of the superficial is barren because it is ultimately always unsuccessful. On the other hand embracing the whole of our human experience is creative. Life may sometimes be painful, but it is the creative pain of birth, which paradoxically connects us with our seat of joy.

My project, *The Search for the Deep Self*, was my attempt to make visible, and celebrate, what happens when we do as Rilke suggested, and you can read eight of the stories from the project in the appendix on page 139. What happens when we live from our deepest core? Through entering the circle of banners and reading the stories, visitors to the exhibition were actually able to meet with people who were willing to share how that process had affected their lives in a creative way.

My story is missing from the banners. This book mitigates that gap. It documents my own search for the deep self, what I found during that process and how I found it. It feels important to me to share my own story in this way as others have shared theirs with me.

Chapter 2
An Archaeology of the Soul

All of our experiences, all our successes and failures, deposit layer upon layer of soil within our souls. In the next few chapters, I tell my story to show the soil in which my art and work grew.

I was born in Ndola, a town in the Zambian copper belt. At that time the country was called Northern Rhodesia and was part of the British Commonwealth. My grandparents had moved there, with two of my mother's three siblings, after the Second World War. A short while later, my mother and brother joined them. Although my mother had just divorced, she was expecting a child: that child was me.

Although I was living with my mother and grandparents, I spent most of my first two and a half years at a distance from the white adults and their dramas. My brother and I were in another world, cared for and protected by our nanny Hester and her husband, the 'houseboy', Zak. In the morning, Hester washed and dressed us, at mealtimes we were fed at a special children's table. During the day we stayed with them while they did their housework. The day ended with Hester bathing us and getting us ready to say goodnight to our parents. When I was with Hester and Zak, I was allowed to dream, to play, to sleep in the shade of a mango tree and to stare through the leaves at the huge blue sky. They lived at the bottom of the garden in a hut with an earth floor and an outside tap. Sometimes I went and sat with Hester outside her hut. I played in the sand with pebbles while she pummelled mealies into flour with a rounded stick and a huge wooden pot. Hester was very large, warm and beautiful, with glossy black skin. She always dressed in bright, pressed cotton and wore a head scarf. Her hips and bottom were so round that they made a kind of ledge on which I perched when she carried me. Somehow I knew that Zak was considered very lucky to have such a buxom wife and that, because of her ample curves, her bride price had been very high. I loved and trusted her and Zak completely.

Everything in Africa was exaggerated. Night came from one moment to the next. Locusts could land in clouds and devour the garden. The heat and the wildness of nature with its myriad creatures meant that it was not possible just to go out and walk. Every journey had to be planned with care. But we children lived outside, with the air on our skin, in wide spaces surrounded by vivid colours. We did not shelter when it rained, but ran out into it to play, even though it sometimes turned to hail, falling with ice stones as large as eggs. Until I moved to England the only shoes I remember wearing, except for very special occasions, were flip flops or tennis shoes. Most of the time we were barefoot, wearing only little cotton shifts or shorts.

We had a treehouse near Hester and Zak's hut, in a grove of mango and avocado trees. It was only a platform up in the branches but I could lie there all day reading and dreaming. The ground below was white and sandy. We made towns and countries with sand, pebbles and twigs.

The big house where my mother and grandparents lived was at the top of the garden. It was large and cool with polished floors and a roomy veranda. My grandmother's budgerigars were kept in a cage by the veranda window and were often surrounded by wild budgies clustering on the net, trying to reach the excited caged birds. As a child I, unlike my grandmother's budgerigars, could choose the wild. I could walk out of our civilized and greened garden into wild scrubland. There I would come across groups of

Africans living in makeshift shanties. They were poor and ragged but they would welcome me and share their food. I spent hours with them, searching for flame lilies and throwing stones at the pawpaw trees to bring down the fruit. Nature was not tame. My brother and I learned this as we stumbled across snakes and fled for our lives. We watched as white, hairy wolf spiders fell from the thatched roof of my grandmother's *rondavel*.

During the weekends or holidays Hester and Zak handed us back to our family. While the grown-ups sat drinking or eating, swimming or playing tennis, we circled them like small planets. There on the green, mown lawns and amid the lush gardens we were witness to what seemed to be a life of never-ending cheerfulness, of plenty and of pleasure. Everything was beautiful and our every need was met by quiet and deferential servants dressed in pressed white uniforms.

The community in which I lived perched on the surface of the real Africa. They had taken their patches of land and made them green and familiar. Right there in the middle of all that wildness we remained resolutely safe and superficial. We were next to nature with all its power and vastness, completely undomesticated and dangerous, but this was nothing more than the backdrop to our lives, something which we mainly ignored.

We perpetuated this uncomfortable tension between wild and caged whenever we left our immediate home – and we often went on holidays. Sometimes we went to the game park where we stayed in thatched *rondavels*, each with a perfect pool and each looked after by its own houseboy. In the morning the pool would be filled with wild otters. During the day we explored the bush. We saw zebra, giraffes, buck of every sort, even rhinos. Sometimes a solitary black figure would emerge from the low, dry brush: immensely tall and dressed in traditional clothes. Sitting in the car, protected from the reality of the bush, it was extraordinary to see someone who didn't need that protection, who knew how to navigate what we feared. They passed by paying us no heed but

17

leaving me feeling honoured to have glimpsed them.

I remember once staying in a beautiful thatched hotel out in the bush. My brother and I left the grounds and climbed a rocky outcrop where we came upon a cave which seemed to contain a kind of altar. There were paintings on the walls, and it exuded an atmosphere of such ancient holiness that we found ourselves becoming still and quiet. It was as if Africa with all its old history broke through everything familiar and showed its face. This event affected me deeply. A deep, soulful music swept away the thin patina of white civilization so that the real country beneath that paper thin colonial world could reassert itself. Another rich reality, layered with history, was asking to be heard. However, when we went back and eagerly told the adults what we had found, no one was interested. The African people with their ancient culture, their stories and languages, their needs and feelings were invisible except as people who could be paid a minimum wage to attend to our comfort. The country with its ancient history was unimportant except as a place with a good climate where our lives could be played out.

· · · · · · ·

The adults also perched on the surface of their inner lives. Not very far below the surface of their distractions, I sensed that something else was going on. Most of the grown-ups we knew came from the same generation as my grandfather, who had been taken prisoner at the battle of Arnhem and spent months in the hands of the Nazis. They had all come to Africa after a hard war. Many of their friends had been prisoners of war in Japan. The wives of these men had endured their own hard times. They'd looked after their children alone in difficult or dangerous situations. Often relationships had been rocked badly by wartime affairs.

I couldn't help but notice that these seemingly competent and cheerful adults were in fact suffering. In moments of quiet when they did not think they were observed, they would look stricken and sad. However, they had no name for their condition. They didn't feel they had any right to be troubled. After all, they had survived. When I asked my mother why they were so unhappy she became so angry, I felt I'd stepped on a landmine. I was confused by her reaction but I couldn't help myself. I couldn't ignore the flashes of pain and anxiety I saw around me or stop caring about what they were all actually feeling.

I had a very good relationship with my grandfather whom I loved to distraction. He allowed me to sit on his knee and sip his beer. I teased him and deafened him by kissing his huge ears. If it was his birthday and we sang for him, he wept; if we had to say goodbye after a long holiday, his eyes filled with tears. But if one or other of us children left food on the side of our plate my warm-hearted grandfather became white with rage.

I only understood this much later when my grandfather was a very old man developing Alzheimer's. Then, having lost his short-term memory, he began for the first time to talk to me about the past and especially about the war. He described being marched across Europe after his capture at Arnhem. Local women had tried to give the prisoners of war food and drink as they passed, and he wept as he told me how the offered comforts were kicked away by their escort. He was angry because he'd known what it was to starve. He was nearly ninety before he spoke of these things. Not even my grandmother had heard these stories.

My grandfather ran away to Australia as a young man, shocking his family by becoming a car mechanic, marrying an Australian girl from the outback, and bringing her back to England before the outbreak of the Second World War. My grandmother was the beloved matriarch of the family. She was a rough diamond with a very earthy way of speaking and a hint of the outrageous. She would say, "Don't sit like that, I can see your breakfast." She fed us brains on toast, kidneys and tripe and onions. With her, people ate and drank too much and did things that they shouldn't. They told risqué jokes, they gossiped and they laughed to deflect anything serious.

Still, between the parties and the laughing, I sensed my grandmother's abject terror that life could be disrupted by some calamity over which she had no control. Her husband had gone to war telling her he would be home in a few weeks; his war had lasted seven years. Right into her old age, when she heard that someone had given birth to a daughter she'd say, "Be glad of daughters – they don't go to war!" For her, life was so fragile at any moment calamity could strike. There was only one solution for this awful state of affairs and that was to eat, drink and be merry.

My mother took part in all this junketing, but she didn't fit in. It was not only her age that made her different. She brought into that suburban, colonial world something of the glamour of the mythical land across the sea – England – which was her real home. Her walls were decorated with Picasso prints and her rooms were furnished with bright Swedish furniture. She was in exile, yearning for her real milieu but cast away in a provincial backwater.

She loved clothes: pretty party dresses and sandals covered in daisies. Her favourite colour was pink. Unlike the rest of the people around her she read everything she could lay her hands on. Still, there was something terribly self-conscious about her. Despite her beauty and her worldly appearance she was hesitant and nervous.

Some of her self-consciousness came from her skin condition. She suffered from psoriasis and, although she always looked lovely, she believed everyone was aware of her patchy skin. She spent every minute she could sunbathing and finding new treatments to treat her symptoms.

Appearance was very important to all the women in the family. They went to the Turkish baths, had their hair done, bought special exercise machines, tried the GI diet and all the others that followed. There was a never-ending struggle to stay slim and beautiful.

Although everyone around me was trying to blot out their inner life and its anxieties, they were unsuccessful. I noticed as a newspaper article ignited an old memory, or as an illness or some seemingly unconnected event would trigger an old concern. It seemed to me that they would seek out more and more tranquillising activities in a desperate attempt to keep these bewildering and overwhelming memories at bay.

If distress were too great to be contained it would be whispered hurriedly, and in secret. I remember, when my mother and I eventually moved back to England, receiving letters from my grandmother and aunt, who were still living in Africa. They described parties and meals, new dresses and the never-ending obsession with their weight. Once, scribbled at the bottom in pencil, my aunt wrote that she was feeling very miserable and couldn't stop crying. She had then added, "Don't tell Nana!" I felt incredibly relieved when I read that little piece of truth. It was a confirmation of what I suspected but could never make anyone acknowledge: that life was far from being absolutely fine.

Not long after this my aunt came to visit. She was a very affectionate person, a great hugger with a lovely dimpled smile. She was not only my aunt but also my godmother. Thinking our affection for each other gave me grounds, I asked her about her sad note. Her sweet face changed into a cold mask and she told me firmly not to talk about what she had written. Even she became cold and threatening at any hint of reality.

They were the saddest, most anxious people one could meet and, although I was a small child, I knew I did not want to be like them. They were surrounded by beauty and a high standard of living; but tragically, because they were uncomfortable in their own skin, their new life in Africa provided no solace. I could see they were all trying to push away their feelings. In order not to be like them I decided to do the opposite. I decided as a very young child that my feelings were precious, and I was determined not to suppress them.

I believe it is very important to allow ourselves to feel. Our whole life of feeling is like a thermometer. Feelings of sadness or happiness, fear and security, discomfort or enthusiasm – all of them bear messages about our inner lives that, when decoded, can help us to understand who we are and how we are responding to the world around us. They need to be felt and explored so that we can understand the questions that our life is asking us.

I remember the first time I consciously chose to feel my own difficult feelings. I was twelve years old and had been sent to boarding school in Malvern, leaving behind my first close friend, Louise. When I came back after the first term I arranged to meet Louise at our old school swimming pool. As I arrived I saw her in the water with lots of girls whom I didn't recognise. As I watched her laughing and talking with all these new people I began to feel utterly miserable. First I was overwhelmed by a wave of loneliness and abandonment. Then I began to feel jealous. I found this very uncomfortable because I didn't like to think of myself as a jealous person. I prepared to push the feelings away and ignore them. Then I remembered my resolution to feel my feelings. Instead of struggling and fearing my feelings I decided to just watch them arise and see what came up. Firstly I saw that my love for Louise had made me very vulnerable. I then saw that I was capable of feeling very jealous. With difficulty I accepted the feelings as part of me. Through doing this I expected to fall into an even deeper state of discomfort and unhappiness. To my astonishment what followed was very positive. As I allowed my feelings to emerge they gave way to a memory. I saw myself back at *my* new school, also in a swimming pool and also with lots of girls whom Louise didn't know. As I thought about this I saw that even though I too had many new friends they had in no way replaced my old friend whom I still loved very much. Looking at Louise, I realised if I could have new friends and still love my old friend, then so could she; all my feelings of jealousy were dissipated in the face of understanding.

When I resolved to feel my feelings and observe them without censoring them, I did not know that I would reach that point of understanding, and therefore liberation. I feared rather that I was going to find out all sorts of awful things about myself. As I passed from abandonment to jealousy I somehow kept my nerve and endured what I was feeling without turning away or closing them down. I then passed through shame and humiliation and still I managed to stay with this unpleasant experience of my inner life. Only by bearing the whole gamut of these feelings, and accepting they were a part of me, was I able to move into the second stage of the process and reach a point of understanding my experience of watching my friend in the pool with all her new friends. Now I had gained something greater than what I had before. I could rejoice that we were both able to love more people, whilst remaining loyal to each other.

Chapter 3
Dark Clouds Gather

One weekend when I was nearly three, I was taken to the golf club by my grandparents and mother. As we sat around the pool a tall man with freckles swam up to us, pushing a large black tyre tube in front of him. If I had to choose music to dramatize this part of my story I would choose the song *Mack the Knife*. The man had a smiling face but his smile was not kind. I had never met him before, but I found myself being handed down to him. This complete stranger put me into the rubber ring and began to push me around the pool. At one end was a huge lion's head out of whose mouth there gushed a stream of water. The man pushed me under it. I howled from the shock of being suddenly drenched in water. He laughed. I was taken to the side of the pool and handed back to my family.

This was my introduction to Freddie Stewart, who was to become my stepfather. I don't remember the details of how he married my mother, or when he moved in. Those early years dreaming under a mango tree just seemed to dissolve into a new life with Freddie in it, and for the next six years we lived with him. Since I was so young when I met him, I grew up thinking he was my father.

Although the people around me were suffering, they were not consciously cruel. Freddie, on the other hand, was not only damaged; he was dangerous.

He loved to dominate and intimidate others. He began with

Zak. I once came into the kitchen and, sensing that something was wrong, I stopped in the doorway and stood very still. I watched as Freddie furtively poured some whisky down the sink. I continued standing at the door, unable to move. Freddie then called Zak out of the larder and accused him of stealing the whisky. Zak's face drained of colour. All the alcohol bottles in the house were marked to prevent pilfering. Freddie was toying with Zak, accusing him of stealing so that he could enjoy his fear and helplessness. As quickly as it had started, he brought the row to an end. The game was over. This time, he let Zak off the hook. In that moment I lost some of my innocence. It was my first encounter with evil.

Zak was entirely dependent on Freddie's goodwill. His job gave him somewhere to live and enough to feed himself and his family. If he was sacked without a reference, it would be very hard for him to get another job. I was only a small child but I found it deeply shocking and painful to see a grown man so afraid. When I saw how Freddie treated Zak, I knew that my stepfather was a bad man, and I was deeply ashamed of being associated with him. Like Zak I was completely powerless. Very soon I realised that I was also a target for Freddie's sadism. He had a small white dog called Magda. I had never had anything to do with dogs before so, although she was harmless, I was frightened of her barking and jumping up on me. As soon as Freddie noticed this, he started to take pleasure in exposing me to the dog so that he could watch me panic. I began to plan strategies to avoid meeting him in the mornings before he went to work. I would wake early and creep across the garden to take refuge in the tree house until he was gone. It was easy to climb up the big, smooth branches of the mango tree and feel safe. Within days, Freddie noticed I was not around to torment and one morning, as I sat quietly waiting for the all clear, he appeared and climbed up onto the platform with a gloating smile. I realised that I couldn't escape him. I would dread waking in the morning, knowing that every day was a battle to get through without attracting Freddie's attention. I remember Zak looking at me with a look of pained concern and compassion. I felt how he cared for me and wanted to protect me. He felt sorry that I too had to live with Freddie's cruelty.

Freddie's sadism was universal. When driving in the bush, he would pretend to stop to pick up a hitchhiker and then speed off laughing just before they got into the car. At the club, he would sit and drink and tell war stories. He had been a gunner on the planes that blanket-bombed Germany. He told us with great glee how, on the way home from bombing raids over Germany, he had gunned down civilians in the countryside. The people sitting around him would laugh and look at him with admiration. Before long, he started to become physically abusive. Once a week my mother spent the afternoon at the Turkish baths. Freddie would come home and wake me from my siesta. He took me to their bedroom and sexually abused me.

As time went on he became more and more reckless. He no longer waited until we were alone. At my grandmother's house I had a bedroom with nothing but a gauze blind and a curtain separating it from the veranda. Even there, with the whole family sitting a few feet away on the other side of the blind, he came and used me.

I hated the abuse, I hated lying beside his hot male body, but I was not powerless. I remember discovering that I was able to take flight and float away just for the time he had me in his grasp. I seemed to be high in the corner of the room looking down. I remember thinking, 'You can touch my body but you can't touch me.' I was very young and small but the abuse led me to an inner part of myself that had a kind of sovereignty way beyond my years.

Side by side with this emerging sense of my own being there was seemingly contradictory experience. In order to protect his secret, Freddie often crept up on me. I would be playing in the garden and suddenly sense he was behind me. He whispered in my ear, 'Never tell or I will kill you.' His threatening tone made me feel I was bad. I thought if I ever gave away the secret I'd be doing something terribly wrong. Although on one level I felt strong this distortion left me feeling confused and disorientated. These tensions between truth and disclosure, between power and victimhood were to become major themes of my life.

• • • • • • •

While we were living there, Northern Rhodesia gained its independence and became Zambia. Freddie, my mother, my brother and I moved to Southern Rhodesia, the adults no doubt preferring the security of living in a British colony. My family's anxiety led me to fear that when we left I would be leaving Zak and Hester in danger. I wanted to help them and so I offered Zak my pocket money, which he refused to take. Instead he smiled and told me kindly not to worry about him. I only realised later that this man who always protected me was probably relieved to be free of us.

Our new house was bright and airy, covered in bougainvillea and surrounded by a large garden. Once again, there were servants dressed in white, polished wooden floors and regularly cooked meals. I was now going to school and no longer looked after by a nanny, and the houseboy didn't live in the grounds. This meant that whenever my mother was out of the house, and my brother was away at school, I would find myself alone with Freddie. This gave him his chance to play out his sadistic and abusive games with no fear of being discovered. Unfortunately on one of his work trips he found a discarded leather whip, used by the Africans to herd animals. It was called a *sjambok* and was a pale creamy colour with a thick sinewy knot at the end near the handle. It was strong and flexible and I remember him walking about the house, bending it ominously. He was a master of both physical and mental torture. Just seeing him holding it and smacking it against his leg put me in a state of high anxiety.

He often used the whip. On one occasion, whilst my brother

Jeremy was home for the holidays, I used my crayons to draw on the wall of my parents' bedroom. When Freddie found the drawings, he came to fetch me from the garden. He brought me into the house and stood over me with the whip, demanding that I confess that the drawing was mine. I was far too frightened to own up. I wept bitterly, denying it was me. He then brought Jeremy into the room and said if I didn't admit it we would both be beaten. I can still see my brother's face streaming with tears and begging me to own up. But I was so terrified that even my brother's pleading couldn't persuade me to deliver myself into the hands of this monster. I was prepared to say or do anything if it meant Freddie wouldn't beat me with the whip. Because I wouldn't confess, we were both eventually made to kneel over my bed while he whipped us.

I ask myself now where my mother was in all this. I don't remember her being there when these things were happening. I can't imagine she would have allowed us to be beaten if she had known. I have only one memory of going to her for help. I told her about a man who kept stopping me and a friend outside our school. He sat in his car with his genitals exposed and asked us repeatedly to get in. When I told my mother about this she seemed embarrassed but not particularly worried. She told me to take his registration number the next time he stopped us. The next day when he turned up, I told him my mother had asked me to write down his number. He sped off and we never saw him again. My mother must have reported this story to my stepfather, who became particularly threatening, implying it was a fiction. I think he believed that I'd made up this story as a way of telling her about him.

Freddie was a good sportsman and an amusing raconteur. Everyone seemed to admire him, including my grandparents. Behind his impregnable image, the secret world between us remained completely hidden. He had a way of pouncing on me with a kind of triumphant relish when he caught me in small

29

misdemeanours, like forgetting to bring my bike in or climbing on to the table to reach a bowl of pudding. It was as if he had thwarted a great crime. This affected me deeply. The abuse, the threats, the assumption that I was up to no good, and the constant punishments meant that I began to experience myself as vile. Standing in assembly at school with other little girls my age I had no sense that I was like them. I too must have been a small girl, neatly dressed in my uniform with my hair ribbons tied and clean shoes and socks but I didn't feel like that. I felt I was different: large and ungainly, besmirched and ugly.

During this time I did something very strange which, I can see now, showed that I still retained some capacity to resist the tyrant. One day I returned home from school to an empty house. Before my parents returned, I went to the kitchen and mixed custard powder and water into a thin solution. Using a doll's drinking bottle filled with the pale yellow liquid, I walked around the house and made tiny patterns until I had marked all the shiny wooden floors with my own intricate song lines. I built these patterns into a complex network of shapes and designs that covered every available surface. By the time the grown-ups came home I was well out of the way with all the tools of my actions washed and returned to their place.

For several days my parents found these inexplicable marks all over the house. I was not included in any discussions about the mystery but I heard the grown-ups talking. My mother especially was very frightened. Eventually a policeman was called and I was asked if I'd seen anything when I returned home from school that could explain the strange marks. When I said I'd seen nothing, everyone believed me. But the arrival of the policeman scared me enough to make me stop my strange behaviour. Although I can't recall ever having a conscious reason for making the marks, I do remember feeling thrilled that I'd managed to execute my plan and, for that brief moment, been able to mystify and alarm those powerful grown-ups.

Chapter 4
Breakdown

At this time, my grandparents were still living in our old home country: Zambia. We went to visit them in what had been Livingstone and, as usual, we went to see the Victoria Falls. On all our previous visits my brother and I had been alone with our mother and grandparents but, this time, Freddie came with us. Occasionally as we walked along the paths we stopped and stood very near the edge of the chasm to watch the dramatic flow of water. At one point, as Freddie, my mother and I stood there looking at the surging water below, the air suddenly became charged with danger. I found myself thinking my own thoughts and, at the same time, I somehow knew very clearly what my mother was thinking. We were both saying to ourselves: he is going to kill us. Without exchanging a word, we clasped hands and stepped away from the side. When we walked on we stayed well away from the edge. We feared that if we didn't move away to safety Freddie was going to push us over.

My mother and I never spoke about this incident, and for years I wondered if I had imagined it. But long after my mother died, my real father told me, to my amazement, that my mother had told him about Freddie wanting to push us into the Victoria Falls. I hadn't imagined it after all.

I know now that this event coincided with the final breakdown of their marriage. It would have been much more convenient to get rid of us by pushing us to our deaths than to have to go through all the expense of a divorce.

· · · · · · ·

William Wordsworth says that children are born 'trailing clouds of glory'[4] – that we bring with us a memory of the realm from where we have come. In those years with Freddie I became aware of those clouds of glory. When the abuse started, I learned that I was able to dissociate from what was actually happening – 'You can touch my body but you can't touch me'. Over time, and whenever things got particularly difficult, I began to have another experience that seemed to be connected with a distant memory rather than a response to a trauma. The memory consisted of a vast and welcoming space and I was quite certain that this memory was a recollection of where I had come from before I was born. I started to see myself standing with my back to a fathomless space floating like a cloak around my shoulders. Since being with Freddie was very frightening, this space became very important to me. It had the quality of a gateway. I believed that it was not only where I'd come from, but also where I could escape to if things became too much. I believed my participation in life was optional, and if I wished I could choose to leave. All I had to do was to turn round and go back through the gateway, the space just behind me. I sensed it was huge, but this didn't make me frightened. It was familiar and welcoming. This conviction that I could escape meant that I never felt totally overwhelmed by Freddie. Being able to leave, I didn't feel entirely powerless.

The run up to my mother's second divorce was a particularly horrible time. Freddie became even crueller and I did my best never to cross his path. However, one day he came home early, before I'd managed to hide. He found me playing in the garden and came up to me. In such a low voice that I couldn't hear him, he began giving me things to do. This was one of his tactics. I knew that if I did the wrong thing because I'd misheard him, he'd have an excuse to punish me. I was suddenly overwhelmed with a great weariness. By then, Freddie and my mother had begun to quarrel openly. I was already terrified by their raging exchanges and this new threat was the last straw. I decided to exercise my power; I chose to leave, to return to my origin.

To my horror, when I turned round to go, I found there was no gateway behind me, no refuge to which I could return. I'd turned around to walk away from my life and found myself instead confronted with nothing more than an ordinary pear tree in an ordinary garden. At first, I panicked. There was no door out. That welcoming space behind me was not there after all. It only existed in my imagination.

Unable to go out and away as I planned, I did the only other thing open to me: I went deeper inside. This was the first time that I truly inhabited my body. Until then, I felt I was hovering between out there and in here, always keeping my options open. Strangely, as I fled into myself, I stumbled onto an equally huge inner space, not *behind me* but *within me*. I had discovered my soul.

At that moment, I found that my origins were not only out and away; they were also within. This meant that although I couldn't walk away I still had options. I was not just what I appeared – a vulnerable little girl. I was much more. I had access to an inner country which was entirely my own. There I was sovereign; there I was free.

There and then I decided that I no longer needed to escape. Instead I would endure and keep walking doggedly forward into life, safe in the knowledge of this inner country. This decision to endure, this awareness of my world of soul, and my earlier decision to feel my own feelings became my North Star. Although I knew that I was surrounded by danger, I had inner resources which helped me find my way through.

• • • • • • •

Suddenly, Freddie left. All the rows and weeping that began soon after our move from Northern Rhodesia ended in his departure.

Until the breakdown of her marriage to Freddie, I had never spent a lot of time alone with my mother. When Freddie left, with my brother at boarding school and the family infrastructure dissolving, we were suddenly thrown together. She fell apart and I became her comforter and confidante. Her despair was overwhelming. Whenever she was at home she sat and wept and drank, while I tried to comfort her with hugs and reassurance. In order to give her hope I would sing popular songs in my tuneless voice. The words of those sentimental songs were my promises that someone would come and rescue her.

My mother and Freddie still had to meet occasionally, to negotiate the divorce. He continued to be cruel and vindictive, finding new ways to wound her. Having betrayed her, he now taunted her. He told her that because of her skin she had always disgusted him. He also refused to pay her alimony which meant she was very worried about money. Freddie's dark side had, up until then, been hidden from her. Now she discovered that he'd always been unfaithful. She was dislocated and broken. Divorce had much more painful implications in those days. She became a symbol of everything everyone in her world dreaded: a twice-divorced woman with no money and two children. She lost all her status and her security. She was utterly humiliated.

One night, some time after Freddie's departure, my mother returned home more distraught than ever. Her divorce had come through that day and she was particularly upset. I sat with her on the sofa, doing my best to help her. I remember feeling drowned in tears and brandy. Eventually she was exhausted and we both went to bed.

Soon after falling asleep, I woke up with a strong sense that I must go and wake my mother. I went to her room and tried to rouse her. She moaned but remained unconscious. As I was sitting with her the phone rang. It was her doctor calling to check up on her. He must have feared for her, knowing the significance of the day. When I told him that my mother wouldn't wake up he told me to wait with her while he called for an ambulance. I had no idea what my mother's symptoms meant but I felt incredibly relieved someone competent had taken control of the situation. Later I learned that she had taken an overdose. If I hadn't been up already I would not have heard the phone from my room and she would have died. My grandparents were informed and I was collected while my mother was rushed off to hospital. The doctor's call had saved her life.

No one sat down and talked to me. I just gathered what had happened through hearing the grownups talk. A day or two later, we went to collect her from the hospital. She got into the car as if nothing had happened and we drove her home. I'd moved in with my grandparents and, for the time being, I remained with them.

• • • • • • •

Eventually my mother moved into a small flat. I was expected to join her there when she was ready and so I was taken to see her new home. As we walked into the flat I noticed a bag of onions sitting on the kitchen table. They had begun to go bad. For me, this single brown bag of decaying vegetables represented the bleak emptiness of the space and my mother's despair. I felt a wave of horror and panic. I knew I couldn't live alone with her again.

Some days later she came to collect me to take me back to live with her permanently. When she was ready for us to leave I could not be found. I'd taken refuge under my grandmother's bed. No amount of persuasion could induce me to emerge from my hiding place. My mother and grandmother tried to drag me out by my feet but I held onto the bed legs and screamed until they gave up and let me stay where I was.

It was then decided I could live with my grandparents. I knew that my mother was hurt that I didn't want to live with her but I just couldn't bear it. Although it was a relief for me that Freddie had gone, life wasn't any easier with my mother, and being with my grandparents meant being left alone to play, it meant being a child. I was no longer being abused whilst under the care of my mother, but I was carrying the responsibility of her pain. Even before the drama of the divorce I often found myself in this role, rubbing her skin with tar ointment, rescuing her from spiders or mice and soothing her when she was sad. My mother was someone I helped, not someone who helped me. For the moment, it was too much. I had to get away from her.

Chapter 5
Boarding School and England

My situation was soon to change once more. My mother decided to leave for England, and it was decided that my brother and I should go to the same boarding school outside Salisbury, Rhodesia, not far from my grandparents.

As a result of the Rhodesian bid for independence, Britain had imposed sanctions on the country. The resulting shortage of petrol meant that while we were at school we had no visitors, nor could we go home to my grandparents for weekends. My new school was divided into the schoolhouse where we all learned together, and two boarding houses where we were separated into boys and girls. I was badly shaken up by this move. I had just come out of a traumatic family breakdown and I had been through too many changes. My schooling had been disrupted several times and it was difficult to have to begin somewhere completely new again. I remember weeping with my class teacher because I felt so cast adrift and rootless; I had no idea where everyone I was familiar with was, or when I would ever see them again.

Boarding school is an initiation in group dynamics. There were constant outbreaks of fighting and weeping amongst the children. The girls were constantly forming and dissolving factions, and I would find myself feeling abandoned and terrified whenever I was cast out of the group. The school punishments were very crude. We had to stand for hours on chairs, or clean our teeth with Lifebuoy soap until our lips swelled and stung. As we slept in dormitories with up to twenty beds there was no peace or privacy, and the food was almost inedible.

My fellow students seemed to have license to behave as badly as they wished. Their dramas and quarrels took up all the space. They had no qualms about being very visible. I was used to children trying to be invisible. Instead of showing embarrassment about their uncontrolled outbursts, they excused every incident with the phrase 'I can't help it; I come from a broken home.' This offended me. I didn't want to give away responsibility for my life in this way. I remember looking at these children and deciding that I would not let what had happened to me give me the excuse for behaving badly. I would choose who I wanted to be.

Not many months after we had been sent to boarding school we were brought home by my grandparents. My grandmother gave me a postcard from my mother. On it was written, 'Mark popped the question, Yes, Yes, Yes!' This was the first time I had heard of my real father's existence. I later gleaned that when my mother returned to England my father's mother had told him that she was there. He was working in Australia, and he took the next plane home. Their divorce had been the result of marrying too young. It was clear that they still loved each other and they remarried very quickly. My brother and I were to return to England to live with them. I was nine years old, and my mother was to come back to Africa one last time to bring us home.

Years later, when I was painting in my studio, I found myself listening to a CD of the first Harry Potter novel[5], not once, but over and over again. At first I was puzzled that I found it so compelling. In the end I realised why it spoke to me so deeply. In Africa I had always felt that I was in the wrong place among the wrong people. The news that I had a real father, and that we were to return to him, confirmed my feeling. This moment in my life resonated with the moment when Harry Potter is told by the giant Hagrid that he is going to be able to leave the Dursleys and go to Hogwarts to be with his own people. Listening to Harry's story, all those years later, enabled me to relive my own unbelievable and utterly wonderful moment of rescue.

• • • • • • •

Although I felt rescued and glad to be going to England, I was also frightened to be leaving my grandparents. I knew I was going very far away and that there would be nowhere to go to if things went wrong at home. In addition, I'd heard the grown-ups talking about Myra Hindley and Ian Brady and what became known as the Moors Murders. I was afraid to go and live in England because I thought it was a place where they abused and murdered children. It never occurred to me that I was already an abused child, and that I myself had already only just escaped being murdered.

We left Salisbury by train and travelled to Cape Town to meet our ship. As soon as we boarded the SS Vaal, my mother retired to her cabin while we explored this floating palace. The contrast with our old life was huge. For me, the luxury was a symbol that we were no longer the beleaguered children of an abandoned mother. Suddenly we had weight and ballast. It felt as if there was a chance of stability. My father joined the boat at Las Palmas.

I expected our reunion to be emotional but instead we were greeted in a very matter of fact way. It was as if we had never been apart. I had no idea what my father was feeling about my brother and me, but I was full of love and admiration. He seemed incredibly beautiful and glamorous.

Arriving in England was a shock. I was amazed at how much clothing we had to wear. Tights and boots, hats and coats. I felt imprisoned in wool. Travelling up the M1 after the empty roads of Africa, and then passing through the Midlands with its cramped housing and urban sprawl was a confrontation with a world I didn't know existed.

When we arrived home I was sent to a small, local public school and, for the first time in my life, I experienced a proper academic timetable. School in Africa had consisted of stories, swimming and tennis. Here, I was behind in everything. I also felt very different next to English children who seemed so pale and sheltered. The huge, open spaces of Africa gave way to a claustrophobic, monochrome world. It took five years before I began to see beauty in England's subtle light and colour.

Whilst my brother and I went to school every day, my mother stayed at home with nothing to worry about but her weight and her psoriasis. She became miserable and bad tempered.

One evening, after reading one of my grandmother's weekly letters from Africa, I made a remark about how horrible Freddie had been. Unwittingly, it seemed that I had brought up a subject my mother had done everything she could to forget. She asked me with what seemed like genuine surprise why I disliked him so much. Remembering the moment at Victoria Falls, and trusting that life with Freddie was something both of us had survived, I told her about Freddie's secret abuse of me. Her reaction was harsh and impatient. She looked at me with something like hate and said with utter contempt, 'These things happen to everyone'.

At that moment I knew that although we had returned home to our real family, home was not necessarily going to be a safe place for me. My mother's attempts to blot out the recent past were so thorough; it was as if it hadn't happened. The past had become unspeakable for her and I had broken her hidden rule.

It took me many years to understand that the look on my mother's face was not hatred but fear. Fear makes us close down and defend ourselves; it freezes out empathy and compassion. My mother was terrified by what I had told her. She feared that she was going to be reminded of a terrible time when she'd been alone and humiliated. She feared that she'd let me down by not protecting me. She feared that being confronted with those difficult and unprocessed emotions would overwhelm her and rob her of her new-found happiness.

At the time, of course, I didn't understand any of this. I was a child, and what I saw was hate; this led me to believe that I was hateful. I am still affected by that moment. On a cellular level I still hold the conviction that there is something frightful and monstrous about me for having told my secret. I was much more wounded by her rejection of my story than I was by the story itself.

This conversation was a key event in my life. By turning me into the problem, my mother reinforced my fear of telling the truth about what I had experienced. The effect of that reversal of reality was so profound it catapulted me into my own exploration, one that had already begun in Africa. I needed to understand how such a thing could happen. I needed to understand what was true and what wasn't. I did not know it at the time, but these were the very first steps in my path to making meaning from my life.

Chapter 6
The Power of Books

As the years passed, my mother seemed to become allergic to me. Everything I did seemed to madden her. In contrast, my parents had a special bond with my brother. As the firstborn, he'd been the beloved child of their first marriage. My mother's constant irritation with me meant that I was excluded from their close-knit group. With no conventional support at home I turned both to my own friends and to books.

I learned to read in Africa. Our little reading books were produced in England for English children. They were wooden, dull and completely lifeless. Now I am amazed any of us persisted in reading them at all. Every evening my grandfather sat with me while I read him my assigned pages. I saw this as a chore until I discovered that this rather dull exercise was actually the source of the real storytelling I experienced as part of school in Africa. I quickly became competent enough to read for myself. As soon as I had mastered the skill I read and read, beginning with Enid Blyton and continuing with everything I could lay my hands on. The stories I read became the building blocks of the magic world of imagination and the place I really wanted to be.

I had one grown-up ally who remained independent of my mother's influence. Hope Helen Hudson was my English grandmother. She lived in a village in Kent in a house that smelled of beeswax, and which was full of art and books. She was not afraid of spiders or ghosts, nor was she afraid of death. She could speak

French. The first book she gave me was *Anna Karenina*[6]. In it she wrote: 'I was given this at your age, I hope you love it as much as I did, Gran.' She also lent me books from her own library. Her one condition was that they must always be brought back. When my grandmother had a tea break with her cleaning lady, Mrs Curtis, I'd sit with them by the aga in her kitchen. They'd smoke and talk about Mrs Curtis's daughter who was radical and interesting and read The Guardian. It was the first time that I had heard people talking about politics as if it was people, not money, that mattered.

My grandmother had worked in publishing and edited the work of Katherine Mansfield. When I stayed with her, I met her female friends. On the dot of six they would pour a whisky and sit down around the fire. They reminisced about the war, which had been a time of liberation for them. They'd been amongst the first women to wear trousers. They went to the pub to play darts, and they had love affairs. They talked about people, ideas, books and poetry. They were dynamic, gossipy and fun.

My grandmother constantly told me that I was marvellous. Her love surprised and touched me. I was deeply grateful to have been returned to England, and to her. I felt tended by her; I knew that she wanted to protect me and help me to grow. Her library became very important to me. Good books about real life are maps which enable us to navigate an alien world. Such books transformed my life.

I had my first experience of the power of books when reading *Where Angels Fear to Tread* by E M Forster. In this seemingly light novel, two young people were despatched to Italy by a conventional English family. Their mission was to rescue the child of a daughter of the family who had made an unsuitable marriage to an Italian. The daughter had since died and the grandchild was to be returned to her respectable English family. While they were there, the young woman who was part of the rescue party began to doubt whether they were doing the right thing. She saw how the child was loved in her Italian family, and she doubted whether respectability was more important than love. The man she was with tried to put her mind at rest and implied she was taking the issue too seriously. She was not convinced and answered him: 'I feel you ought to fight it out...Every little trifle, for some reason does seem incalculably important today, and when you say nothing hangs on it, it sounds like blasphemy. There is never any knowing which of our actions, which of our idlenesses won't have things hanging on them forever.'[7]

Those words woke something up in me. I had been living in a kind of trance. I didn't feel connected to myself or my life. A thick, opaque layer had formed between me and the world, made up of the superficial and numbing leisure culture of colonial Africa, its resistance to thinking about anything difficult, and its sense that our lives and our way of living had neither significance nor responsibilities. I was disorientated and confused, as if something important was lying just out of my reach. I knew that I needed to grasp whatever this 'something important' was.

Until I read Forster's story I feared that the values of my upbringing were true, and that all that mattered was having enough money and keeping happy and distracted. This book allowed a different reality to trickle through the conventions I'd grown up with. Forster was saying that the human drama does matter. His words cut through my stupor. When I applied his values to my life I saw that for want of these values, I was depressed.

I fed this fragile new consciousness as I would have done a seedling. I now knew that there were people who believed in a deeper reality (in this case, love) and thought it was worth fighting for. That reality was not mystical or other-worldly; it was simply reality – all I needed to do to attain it was to practise acknowledging what was really happening, rather than avoiding it.

Gradually I found out about other authors who'd written truthfully, from the heart. They became my allies, and just like Forster and his writings, they stopped me from feeling alone and gave me the confidence to endure my childhood. I resolved that as soon as I grew up I would go out into the world and find people like them.

My grandmother died only a few years after our return to England. When my father told my brother and me of her death, I was so shocked that I cried out. My strong emotions frightened my brother who promptly told me to shut up. Her death was not discussed again. Later I found out from my mother that Gran had suffered a stroke and died very suddenly. By the time I learned she was dead, she had already been cremated. She had disappeared from the face of the earth. Later I grieved and wept alone – I'd lost my only ally in the family.

At the end of our last visit to her, I had gone up the steps from her garden to get into the car. As I reached the car I had a strong feeling I should go back again. I walked back down the steps that led to her front door and found her standing there, as if expecting me to return. We hugged and kissed and I told her I loved her. She smiled at me and said, "I know." I never saw her again.

After her death we moved into her house. The aga was disconnected and taken away. It was considered too expensive. We were living in her beautiful space but its warm heart had been ripped out.

• • • • • • •

When I was twelve years old, I was sent to Malvern Girls' College. The school had a reputation for valuing the education of young women and fostering their self-belief. Until the sixth form, we lived in school houses, each with their own names and traditions. One evening, while we were all changing shoes in the cloakroom, I saw a small freckled girl with thick red plaits turn on another member of our group. Her target's eyes filled with terror. I decided that I was not going to let her be victimised. I didn't feel brave; I simply couldn't cope with the idea of once again living with someone I feared. To my amazement when I stood up to the bully, she immediately backed down.

At my previous boarding school in Africa, the girls had been constantly divided by quarrelling factions. My initial run-in with the red-haired bully suggested that Malvern might be the same. Standing up to her successfully was a turning point for me. By making myself visible in this way, I connected with other girls who wanted to have a different kind of relationship. We discovered that we could influence how we treated each other and so we resolved to try and change the dynamic between us even more. By deciding to be open and honest, as well as kind and supportive, we had a real impact. Together we were able to warm a small part of the world, creating a microclimate in which trusting friendships could flourish. To a large extent, the quarrelling and division into factions dissipated. Instead it became normal, at least for some of us, to share our problems and to express affection.

Our housemistress noticed that our group was unusually close but our intimacy unsettled her. It was her job to manage the house community. I believe that she feared that our mutual support might make it harder to control us.

As we got older we became more aware of politics. It was the time of the Vietnam War, and an American girl in our group told us about the Women's Peace Movement in the USA. I had also begun reading about the imprisonment of the Soledad Brothers and Angela Davis. At the back of the book was a form to join their defence campaign. Reading the story of these African-American activists triggered my memory of the way Freddie had treated his servants. I wanted to express my concern regarding their mistreatment. I also signed up for the peace campaign. Before long, newsletters from both campaigns started arriving at the school. These issues were very much part of the spirit of the time and I read about them with the same interest as I read novels or poetry, or about the lives of people I admired.

One evening, just as everyone was going to bed, I was called in to see my housemistress in her private sitting room. To my surprise I discovered she had kept back the most recent newsletters. In spite of the fact that both campaigns were legitimate and legal, she asked me why on earth I was getting the school mixed up in these radical issues. When I found that she had been keeping back my correspondence, I was furious and defended my right to receive the letters. As I spoke she became pale and angry and hit me in the face. She then told me that I had been born with the gift of leadership but that I had given my gift over to the devil. I was stunned. She threw my newsletters in the bin and sent me to bed.

The uneasiness and irritation of both my housemistress and my mother when confronted by my friendships, and now my social conscience, affected me deeply. Why would an attempt to be kind and supportive, to think about the world, evoke such strong reactions from the adults around me? I felt that we were like characters in a Grimm's fairy tale surrounded by wicked stepsisters and witches who were angry with us, not because of our weaknesses but because of our sweetness and resilience.

These run-ins with authority became catalysts in the same way as my mother's refusal to engage with our mutual past had been a catalyst. I needed to find out what was so frightening about a group of people who are able to build a community based on openness and trust.

• • • • • • •

Not long after I came to Malvern I was in the junior art block making a poster for a jumble sale. As I painted, a woman came out of the senior art room and leaned over my work. She said to me, "You love painting!" I had no idea what she was talking about until she invited me into the lecture room and showed me slides. I was ravished. From then on I became as obsessed with art as I was with books.

My art teacher, Mrs Howell, was six feet tall, thin as a rake and dressed in beautifully-cut tweeds. She looked like a character from a novel by Radclyffe Hall. Above the doors of her art block were Wordsworth's lines: 'The world is too much with us, late and soon, / Getting and spending we lay waste our powers.'[8]

Mrs Howell was the first teacher who made me feel like she actually believed in what she was teaching us. Although I was receiving a good education, where I was introduced to all the great ideas of civilisation, it felt like an accessory, something we needed in order to integrate successfully into our tribe. It was this that had made me mistrust my housemistress so completely: that she claimed to have values but was actually demanding nothing more than conformity.

Earlier I mentioned Rilke's description of the City of Pain and The Land of Pain. These two ways of looking at the world help to describe the tension of my education. Our religious services took place in an ancient priory with exquisite music, mediaeval windows and readings from the profound texts of the St James Bible and the Book of Common Prayer. At school we were reading poetry, plays and novels by the most accomplished writers of the English-speaking world. In our history lessons we were learning about the brave men and women who had made history and changed the world. The art room was full of book about the lives of artists.

We were immersed in the 'Good and the Beautiful' and my response was to love these ideas, and to assume they had a practical application. Yet I was to gradually realise that for the majority of the adults around me, the knowledge they were imparting was of no more value than the knowledge we needed in order to hold our own at dinner parties.

In Mrs Howell's art block there was none of this tension. In her youth she had taught art to patients in a large hospital for the mentally ill. At the time such work was revolutionary. Because of her husband's work she'd had to move to Malvern. She brought her idealism to our school. She spoke of her former students with admiration. For her they were not the terrifying 'other'; they were not life's losers. On the contrary, she respected them for their fortitude in their illness, as well as their capacity to be uniquely creative. Whilst my first encounter with idealism had been through literature and the history of ideas, the more important encounters were with people. In my grandmother and Mrs Howell, for the first time I met living idealists outside of the pages of books. They were real and I loved them for it. In Erich Fromm's book, *To Have or to Be*, he says:

> Being an authority is grounded not only in the individual's competence to fulfil certain social functions, but equally so in the very essence of a personality that has achieved a high degree of growth and integration. Such persons radiate authority and do not have to give orders, threaten, bribe. They are highly developed individuals who demonstrate by what they are – and not mainly by what they do or say – what a human being can be.[9]

Mrs Howell was such a person. Her students didn't have to be cajoled to come to work and learn. I ran to the studio not only when it was on my timetable but whenever I was free. In every other class we were working to pass exams so that we could get into university. In Mrs Howell's classes we worked because it was wonderful to work, and because we were eager to stretch ourselves and become better painters. She was not interested in our becoming successes in the conventional sense; she was interested in our becoming self-motivating individuals who had found our own visual language.

My pantheon, which began with my grandmother and Mrs Howell, went on to include writers, thinkers, artists; anyone I could find who had lived deeply and recorded what they had learned. Literature and the exploration of ideas were never abstract for me. When I felt disorientated and powerless, marooned without anyone to talk to, the ideas, stories and images I found in books were like messages in bottles that washed up on the shore of the lonely island of my childhood. They described another way of being and living. They gave me a frame of reference for understanding myself and what was happening around me.

My mother had told me that I lived my life as if I was the character in a novel. She meant it as a criticism. It implied that I didn't understand real life. I felt that it was her life that wasn't real and I was encouraged by her criticism. The kindred spirits whom I met in art and literature helped me to disentangle myself from the deathly grip of my childhood.

Chapter 7
University Years

After completing our examinations at the age of sixteen, the Malvern girls were sent in small groups to help people 'less fortunate than ourselves'. I was sent to a Camphill community, to live and work for a week with adults and children with special needs. I was a little afraid because I'd never met a person with special needs before. I expected a huge institution; a place that looked like old pictures of Bedlam. Instead we were taken to a country estate deep in the heart of Gloucestershire. It was a warm day and the community was marking the festival of John the Baptist with an outdoor celebration. After we had dumped our luggage and seen our minibus disappearing down the drive, we were led down into the field where the community had gathered to perform a play. This took place within a circle made up by the people with special needs, who were called 'villagers', and the 'co-workers' who shared their lives with them. Before the play began, there was a short talk about the meaning of the festival. I remember the speaker connecting our daily lives with the rhythms of the seasons and the stars. His reference to our connection to the Cosmos resonated with my own experience of connection to that huge unknown. He seemed to possess wisdom far beyond anything I had ever encountered before. I found myself thinking, 'Here is an adult who really tells the truth.' Although I had never heard these ideas before they didn't seem alien to me. It was more that he was putting into words something I had always known and longed for: that life and *all* our experiences were in fact a meaningful narrative and not something random.

That week we girls had to work. It was the first time I had ever done anything either so useful or so practical. We helped with cooking and we worked in the garden. We were shown what to do on every occasion by the villagers. I remember going into the kitchen on the first morning and being introduced to my two teachers. They were both young women with Down's Syndrome. I was very moved by their open-hearted sweetness and their patient willingness as they showed us what to do.

Our life there wasn't all wholesome and hardworking. When the working day ended we spent the evening with a group of wild boys. They were the children of the full time co-workers who ran the community. Every year they looked forward to the arrival of Malvern girls the way fishermen anticipate the return of the salmon. As night fell they led us across the fields to the local pub and plied us with cider and lemonade. When we got home from the pub we stayed up until sunrise smoking, talking and drinking while they desperately tried to bag one of us. In the course of a week we were introduced to a life of service and a life of sensual pleasure. The combination of the sacred and the profane was intoxicating and we had the time of our lives.

I spent the next two years back at school, doing A levels. Not long ago I came across two books I had been presented with when I left school. They were the sixth form prizes for art and literature. I was very surprised. I had no memory either of winning these prizes, or of being praised for doing so. When I told my mother that my art teacher believed I could be an artist, she said coldly, "Oh everyone has potential." Despite praise and encouragement from my teachers, the active discouragement of my mother blotted out the memory of my successes.

This lack of self-belief and adult support influenced my choice of further education. I applied to study Philosophy and English Literature. I chose Philosophy because I had an inkling that it might have something to do with wisdom. I chose literature because I thought that's where I would find people who lived the deeper life that E M Forster and others described in their novels. Because of my mother's discouraging words, I didn't even imagine I could apply to art school.

I arrived at York University at eighteen, with a kind of study fatigue. Instead of looking forward to learning I found myself thinking, "Oh no, not more being stuffed with knowledge." School had been an exam factory. Not having been taught to learn independently, not having ever managed money nor used public transport, not even knowing how to use a library, I was ill-equipped to make the transition from a sheltered boarding school to a university. Nevertheless I was excited and hopeful that now at last my real life would begin.

· · · · · · ·

The Australian author Miles Franklin wrote two novels about a young woman who wanted to become a writer. In the first one, *My Brilliant Career*[10], the young heroine refuses a rich suitor and a life of ease to pursue her ambition. The second novel, called *My Career Goes Bung*[11], starts as she arrives in Sydney. She expects to be able to live a life of creativity surrounded by equally serious and enthusiastic people. Instead she is confronted by a group of authors and critics devoured by jealousy and ambition and obsessed only with themselves and their aim to get to the top.

I mention these novels because the heroine's experience resonates with mine. At university, I was expecting to meet characters like those I had read about: people wanting to live a deeper life. It was that conviction that had helped me through being a child. This was not the case. Generally speaking, our teachers didn't seem to care for us or for the responsibility of teaching us. On the first day of term the English professor satirised our love of writers and writing. He was weary of naïve young women worshipping Virginia Woolf and the like. Lectures were deadly dull, mostly because the teachers had prepared them years before and simply read out the lecture notes standing at a podium. There were occasional exceptions but they were too few and far between to radically change my experience. Despite their profession, despite their subject matter and role, my teachers seemed as sad and lost as many of those in authority I had met both at home and at school. I felt disappointed and afraid. If the people living a deep life were not here in the literature and philosophy department of a good university, then where on earth were they?

This was not a good time to go to university looking for meaning. Literature at York had once stood under the star of F. R. Leavis, whose book *The Great Tradition*[12] had been written out of his belief that literature and education were there to provide a moral perspective. This was my motivation for reading: to find out what it meant to be human. But by the time I got to York, these ideas had been discarded. Postmodernism with its outright rejection of meaning had become the new orthodoxy. Leavis was considered old-fashioned and paternalistic.

My most enriching experience in York came through meeting the writings of the American Women's Movement. I found myself reading the work of a group of women who had experienced both the Civil Rights Movement and the Vietnam War. For them, the Sixties Revolution had grown up out of real challenges and real suffering which gave their work authority. I came across a book by Judith Arcana called *Our Mothers' Daughters*[13]. Its attempt to find common ground between mothers and daughters inspired me to try to redeem my own sad relationship with my mother. Without her support I felt very exposed and alone. I needed some kind of backing. I needed to know that, although I was up there on the high wire, there was somewhere to fall. The next time I was home, I gave her the book to read. I imagined that she would read it and reflect on our experience of being mother and daughter.

The next time I saw her, I asked her what she thought. I hoped to start a conversation where I could describe my longing to connect with her in a different way. When she answered her face lit up. She thanked me very warmly and said the book had helped her because it made her feel so much better about her relationship with her own mother.

Her answer was so unexpected that I felt dizzy. I realised I simply didn't exist for her as a daughter. I saw that, instead of trying to connect with her, I had to give her away. I needed to see her not as my mother, but as a suffering human being from whom I could expect nothing. I had to stop wanting something from her that she couldn't give, and so I consciously tried to give her away. This was painful, but I could see no other option.

· · · · · · ·

Years later I went on a journey to Auschwitz. There I saw a permanent exhibition in the so-called Sauna: the shower block where the prisoners were taken to be shaved and tattooed. The exhibition, called *Before They Left*, consists of photographs that were found in the suitcases of the victims of the Holocaust. They are hung in groups with as much biographical detail as could be found. The project is an attempt to give names and stories to the anonymous dead.

I found myself unable to stop looking at one particular image. There was no information beneath it. It was a picture of a mother and daughter in their swimsuits. They were in the garden of a country villa. The little girl was about nine – the same age that I had been when I was looking after my despairing mother in Africa. They had their faces turned to each other, so that we could see them in profile like Egyptian hieroglyphs. The mother had strong features and was very beautiful, just as my mother had been when she was young. She was not just looking at her daughter, she was beholding her, and her small daughter was basking in that life-giving look.

I was well into my forties when I saw this image. It connected me to what was, up until then, an unknown longing – a longing I had suppressed in an attempt to accept reality. Although I thought I'd given away any hope of having a mother I had, in fact, never got over realising she was not there for me. She was my wound. She was the place where I was most vulnerable. Whilst other people are constantly looking for the romantic love of their lives, I was always looking for a mother, an older woman who would behold me with that same life-giving, unconditional regard.

The Jungian writer Clarissa Pinkola Estes has written an inspirational book about women and their creativity called *Women Who Run with Wolves*[14]. In it, she uses stories to help women understand themselves and their choices, and to empower them to connect with their own source of creativity. I read this book for the first time in my forties. It helped me to understand myself during my youth. She calls young, unmothered women 'blueberry muffins'. In other words they are soft, sweet and vulnerable. I was just such a girl and, like all such girls, I had to learn not at the knee of a wiser woman but from my own mistakes.

• • • • • • •

My mistakes at university included foolish love affairs and loony left politics. Eventually I retired to bed with depression. All I could do was sleep and read my way through my reading list. We were studying nineteenth century literature. I worked my way through George Eliot, Charles Dickens, Mrs Gaskell and Thomas Hardy. My own story was unravelling but I immersed myself in a kind of storytelling where good is triumphant and evil is overcome. The stories were small pieces of flotsam to which I clung in order to stop myself drowning.

The weeks passed with no change. Every day one of my flatmates would look into my room nervously to bring me my post. One day a letter arrived from a friend who had actually fled her university and was now living in London in much the same state as me. Her letter came in a padded envelope. Sitting up in bed in the half-light I opened it and a tiny Christmas tree decoration fell out – a crudely formed owl made of red velvet and sequins. As the owl fell from the envelope, its sequins flashed in the light that was seeping through the crack in my curtains. The flash of light called up an answering flash in my soul. I reconnected with my inner self and I knew that I could survive the disappointment of both university and my unresolved relationship with my mother. I left my bed and re-joined student life.

Just before the end of my degree something happened which brought to the surface the deep experiences of my early childhood. I was on the way to a philosophy lecture and was worried about being late. I had jumped off my bus and was standing in front of it ready to hurry across the road. Just as I began to walk into the road I heard someone call my name. The voice was faint and high like a bell and seemed to come from a great distance. I immediately stepped back in order to look for who was calling me. My sudden halt caused my bag to swing out in front of me. As it swung out it was bashed by a passing car. If I had not stepped back in response to that invisible voice I would have been killed. I looked all around to see who had called my name. There was no one behind me and there was no one on the bus looking my way. The voice seemed to have come from nowhere. The bus moved off and all I could do was to continue with the day as if nothing had happened.

As I walked on to my lecture everything around me expanded and I found myself connecting anew with that huge, inner space and the accompanying sense of meaning that had been so vivid to me when I was a child. The experience left me with a sense of the fragility of life but at the same time I was reminded, at an existential level, that my life did have some significance, and that I could go on.

On the day I received my degree, I found myself confronted with having to think about what to do with the rest of my life. As everyone around me turned their attention to the real business of living, I began to panic. I was afraid that I would have to go to work somewhere that I didn't really care about. I went to bed that night and found myself offering a prayer to a nameless being. I prayed to find work that I loved so much that I would wake up every morning longing to meet the day. I woke the next morning dreaming of Camphill.

Chapter 8
Finding Community

During my time at university I had never once thought of that week living in community. Reawakened to that experience, I now resolved to go and find out if it would be possible to work there as a long term co-worker. Making art in Mrs Howell's art block and that one week in Camphill had been the happiest times of my life. Walt Whitman tells us to dismiss everything that insults our soul. This is what I now did. I was tired of postmodernism. I was tired of a world view which insisted that there was no growth and development in human history. I dared to believe, despite my lack of any kind of status, that those miserable and uninspiring academics who had dominated our curriculum might be wrong. I decided to take control of my life.

My plan was to go to work in Camphill for a year and then to apply to art school. I wanted to reconnect with my creativity and myself. To my surprise I discovered there was a Camphill Community very near York. A friend offered to take me and introduce me to the founder. His name was Peter Roth and I was astonished to discover he was the same person I'd heard speaking 'the truth' all those years before.

The drive to Botton led us over the North York Moors. As we took the small road that curved from the hilltops down into the valley, I became aware of the slopes stretching up into the sky, like in an exquisite Japanese drawing. The landscape had a beautiful emptiness that filled me with a strange nostalgia. Once again I found myself reminded of that blissful, empty space that had so comforted me as a child. I think one of the reasons I was so drawn to Botton was that it was a physical manifestation of that early memory of a spacious but welcoming doorway back to the realm of my origins. After the barren lessons of university I believed that I had found a Garden of Eden where I felt sure I would be able to live and to flourish.

Peter had suffered from polio when he was a young man which meant he was unable to do physical work. He always spoke about this handicap light-heartedly because, he said, it had freed him up to do what he really wanted, which was to have time for people. I visited him in his office which was painted deep red. On his wall he had a painting by August Macke. It was of people in a sunlit park on the Lake of Thun. The simplified, silent figures painted in blocks of glowing colour had, like certain kinds of music, the power to bring tears to my eyes. I felt convinced that people who had such pictures on their walls must be good.

Peter gave me his full attention. Conversation was for him a means of sharing and revealing what lay on one's heart. I had never met anyone who thought that people and their lives mattered so much and I loved him for it. I shared with him my disappointment with what I'd learned at university. I shared my longing to find a more convincing and inspiring way to think and to live. Somehow I also felt the need to confess that I'd had a painful childhood. I feared I might be in some way irreparably damaged, and I wanted to be honest about it.

He dismissed that thought. He told me that whatever had happened to me, I had a central core that no one could harm and that I would be able to overcome the challenges of my biography. Although I didn't just take this at face value I found myself deeply affected by his words. I loved the idea that I might not be broken because it liberated me from a fear of being hopelessly trapped by the past. I decided to live with the possibility that his words were true and to see where they led me. This conversation ended with

Peter asking me to come and live in Camphill. I agreed, thinking I would live there for a year and then go on to art school. In the event, I was so excited and fulfilled by life in Botton that I stayed for fourteen years.

• • • • • • •

The first Camphill community was established in Aberdeenshire in 1939. The founders were a group of friends in Austria who, being Jewish, had fled the country before the Anschluss in 1938. They found their way to Britain, where they reconnected and resolved to respond to the challenges of their time with a creative act. They were a cultured group, mostly students, deeply committed to living meaningful lives. In the face of the brute power of the Third Reich, they decided to form a community where they would share every part of their lives with so-called 'handicapped children'. This was a significant decision in the light of what was happening in Nazi Germany. There, the handicapped, mentally ill and disabled had been categorised as 'useless mouths' and the Nazis had set up the Euthanasia Project to murder them. They, on the other hand, had a profound respect for these threatened and vulnerable human beings, and they had a passionate commitment to their right to be seen as wholly human. This was an act of defiance in the face of the Nazi ideal of the superman who was praised precisely because he was unhampered by empathy or compassion. Living together with the handicapped would be a statement of belief in the precious humanity of every individual. It would be an act of non-violent resistance in the face of war and an inhuman ideology. By the time I joined the movement, there were over seventy homes, schools and villages on four continents.

When Camphill was first established it was a revolutionary idea. Until then no one had recognised people with special needs as human beings with a right to have a proper education or meaningful work. The founders of Camphill respected the so-called handicapped on many levels. They perceived that the vulnerability and open-heartedness of people with special needs were essential elements in their attempt to create a blueprint for a better world. They saw their guilelessness and vulnerability not as a weakness but rather as strength, the strength to be seen in one's nakedness. This authenticity, this capacity to be themselves, was a vital aspect of the whole set-up. In this sense the role of the children in the community was not to be cared for; rather children and co-workers both helped and learned from each other.

The driving force behind the movement was a man called Dr König. When I went to live in Camphill, I spoke with some of the parents who had met him at the beginning of the first community. They had gone to him in despair. More than one parent described being told at the birth of their child to "put 'it' away. It will only make you unhappy." Dr König was different. He reassured them that, although their children's bodies might be damaged, their essential eternal being was intact.

The first Camphill community was built around children and their need for a proper education. When those children grew up and had nowhere to go, Dr König did not abandon them or their parents. Instead he founded an adult community, where the focus changed from meaningful education to meaningful work. Botton Village was the first such Camphill village. Peter Roth was given the task of establishing it: he saw it as a kind of greenhouse where new ideas about every aspect of life could be incubated. It was his hope these ideas could be taken out into the wider world once they had matured.

•••••••

Between the ages of twenty-one and thirty-five I learned what it was to work and grow in a way that very few people are allowed to experience. I was in love with my life. When a group of people work well together for a common aim they can find themselves growing and becoming more than the sum of their parts.

Like most people living in Camphill, I had a lot of practical work to do. I ran a large craft workshop; I looked after a household (which meant cooking and organising family life); I ran the village gift shop and I edited the journal of the International Camphill Movement. My practical work was the heartbeat of my life. It gave me order and structure and, in a heady atmosphere of idealism, it grounded me. I also worked as a teacher and used my creative skills to help facilitate festivals. Through a deep relationship with an older woman, who was herself an artist, I also learned to give lectures about art and the development of consciousness. I have never worked so hard, and I have never felt so well. I loved living there and I loved being part of making the community happen.

Every year a large group of young co-workers came to live with us. Many of them came because they were experiencing the same kind of crisis that I had. Others were less troubled and came as part of their year off or to learn English, while some came because they were looking for an alternative lifestyle. They started by attending a foundation course, which introduced them to this very different way of life and gave them a chance to study some of the theories behind the project. Despite my youth, Peter put me in charge of this course. I was supported and helped in my work by a small group of older co-workers who had helped Peter found Botton. They were steeped in Middle European culture and they shared their enthusiasm with me. I was introduced to all the great artists, poets and thinkers of the nineteenth and twentieth centuries.

The community was built on the ideas of Rudolf Steiner. His body of thought, called Anthroposophy, can be directly translated as 'the wisdom of man'. Anthroposophy has engendered biodynamic agriculture, Waldorf education, ethical banking, and different forms of painting, movement, drama and special education. Steiner taught that we could develop faculties to connect with the spiritual reality that lies behind the appearances of the material world. Because our lives in community were grounded in practical life, there was nothing other-worldly or mystical about this. The philosophy manifested in respect for all living things. Nature was not seen as something to exploit but something to care for and respect.

Steiner saw history as the unfolding of human consciousness. For him, the purpose of life was to learn to stand in one's own authority and act out of freedom. His world view influenced everything we did in Botton. With the help of the founders, I designed a course taking full advantage of everything that they taught me.

Peter called education the cultivation of soul intelligence. Through the different courses on offer in Botton, he wanted to help the students see themselves and their own time in context. So we studied history from earliest times until the present using art, literature and the history of ideas to observe and discover how consciousness has metamorphosed from age to age. His greatest gift was his interest. His deepest longing was for his fellow community members to become interested in each other. Meeting Peter and seeing him work in this way helped me to find an outlet for my own interest in human beings. Through the course, the teachers and mentors involved were able to help the students find themselves and their vocations both in, and beyond, Camphill. Leading this course taught me to be infinitely flexible. Every new group came with different questions and needs and it was my job to find the right language for each one. Out of this I discovered my own passion for teaching. It was an amazing thing to see a meek and cowed young person find their voice, and their next step in life, through work and learning.

While I was there I became familiar with the whole circle of life. I saw people marry and have children and, in my first year in Botton, one of the older co-workers in my house died. I discovered the community did not hide away from death. Her body was laid out and, for three days, people took turns to sit with her. We came together to speak about her life and then we all went to her funeral. Her illness and her death gave me access to an experience which remains important to me to this day. Death never ceases to challenge and strike awe into my heart but, instead of either dreading or ignoring it, I began to include consciousness of mortality in my life.

Chapter 9
Dying and Becoming

For all its positive qualities, Botton was not without its problems and, as the years passed, these problems began to radically affect our lives. When people applied to join Botton as full time co-workers, there was no formal way of ensuring whether they had identified with its original aims and intentions. This meant that there was no way of holding them accountable to the community's founding purpose. Peter believed that if he loved people enough they would eventually listen to him and support his aims. In time this created a lack of clarity of purpose and a dilution of our ideals. This lack of common purpose was the root of what became a breakdown in communication between the co-workers.

Years later I was able to find the tools to diagnose and describe the issues and behaviours that led to the community losing its capacity to contain conflict and work through it. Before I found those tools, the best I could say was that there was a power struggle which led to a large group of people working in Botton no longer feeling able to identify with crucial aspects of our life. No longer feeling at one with the workings of the community, and at a loss to know what else to do, this group chose to leave. I belonged to that group. For the next two years I lived in the nearby town of Middlesbrough where, in response to a request from the city council, a small group of us tried to establish an urban wing of Camphill.

This failure was no small thing for the people concerned. As I surveyed what I saw as the ruins of my adult working life I felt foolish and washed up. My choice to live in community had been one I had once celebrated. I now had to decide whether I still believed in our capacity to live and work together, or whether I needed to admit that I had squandered my life on an impossible dream.

· · · · · · ·

Most people can call to mind the names they have been called – I call them 'wound words'. Some of us carry these wound words around for many years. They can leave us feeling as if we are somehow in the wrong and not as we should be. I was always told I was too intense. No one I asked could explain what was wrong with being intense. The earnest aspirations of Camphill had given me a home for my intensity. It had not been welcome in my earlier life, and the failure of our community endeavour made me fear it would not be welcome in my future life. I needed to research what this word 'intense' really meant to me, and why it could be the source of such fulfilment for some and the source of such discomfort for others.

Once again, literature came to the rescue, in the shape of Ibsen's *Peer Gynt*[15]. Towards the end of the play, Peer Gynt meets a being called the Button Moulder. He tells Peer that he has come to collect him in order to melt him down for buttons. He explains that Peer has not become a bright shiny button on the waistcoat of life: in other words he has not become the self he could have become if he had taken his life more seriously. Peer Gynt is indignant about this dreadful fate and argues with the Button Moulder. He defends himself by asserting that he has both sinned greatly and loved greatly and, therefore, has a right to be sent either to heaven or to hell but not to be consigned to oblivion. The Button Moulder disagrees strongly with Peer Gynt. He tells him that he has been neither very good nor very bad. Instead he explains he has been so mediocre, it would have made no difference if he had not lived at all.

Peer then asks what he would have needed to do to become the bright, shiny button of his best self. The Button Moulder tells him he should have lived his life more intensely. Peer asks what this means. The Button Moulder explains that in order to live his life more intensely he must learn to die and become. Peer Gynt is very confused by this advice. Nevertheless, the Button Moulder persists, saying that although Peer may find this call to self-transformation difficult to grasp, he should at least *try* to understand it. Peer Gynt's problem has been his inertia about his life, his unwillingness to try. He has given in to incomprehension when he needed instead to see his problems as a challenge to awaken to what his life was asking from him. By failing to at least try to understand his own existence he has failed in the task of self-realisation, which is the primary work of every human being.

The Button Moulder told Peer Gynt that he must live more intensely and that, in order to do that, he must die and become. Goethe also speaks of dying and becoming in his poem, *Blessed Longing*. He says:

> Never prompted to that quest:
> Die and dare rebirth!
> You remain a dreary guest
> On our gloomy earth.[16]

Here, Goethe goes even further than Ibsen and says that only by daring to give oneself to this process can we cease to be strangers, becoming instead truly at home in our own lives. In the English translation the German words 'trüber Gast' have been translated as 'dreary guest'. The word 'trüb' can also be understood in different ways. When referring to weather it can mean hazy. When referring to air or water it refers to a loss of transparency.

Used as an image for our life of soul, it suggests a dimming of our capacity to experience life fully in all its manifoldness.

This reminds me of my state of soul before the epiphany of reading E M Forster's words, 'There is never any knowing which of our actions, which of our idlenesses won't have things hanging on them forever.' Reading those words woke me from a kind of dull trance in which I had believed there was no option but to conform to the norm. As I have already described, my childhood was full of injustice. I lived in a big, clean house with no material needs while at the bottom of the garden an African family lived in a single room with a mud floor and a tap outside the front door. My stepfather's behaviour was quite obviously wrong and yet no-one chose to challenge either our lifestyle or his actions. In my childhood, the only way of being that adults modelled was to shut down one's conscience and to ignore painful realities rather than respond to them as legitimate concerns, as responsibilities. As a result, life felt cold, flat and grey and even as a small child I dreaded that this was all there was to hope for. In my trance-like state I felt as if I was missing some important piece of knowledge that I desperately needed in order to understand my life. This lost key and its consequent lack of clarity left everything blurred.

Forster's words, spoken in the novel by a young woman who believed that how we choose to behave does matter, broke through the blur and cleared the fog. I was able to experience life in a different way, as if my inner eye had been cleared of a dimming mist. My depression lifted and life began to have layers and depth. It regained its savour. I renewed my vow to feel my feelings, and you could say that I embraced intensity. This awakening to life and its meaning is what Goethe encourages us to experience through daring to die and become. I knew as an existential reality what Goethe meant with the expression, 'trüber Gast'. I knew what it meant to be cut off from my real self and my intensity was my antidote to that sterile existence. So my 'intensity' became something I want to celebrate rather than something I am ashamed of, part of the process of dying and becoming.

Peer Gynt was very puzzled by the phrase dying and becoming. Goethe might have suggested that he looked to nature for an answer; he called her the open secret, suggesting that we look to her in order to understand better what is meant by this phrase, not just for nature but also for ourselves. The natural world is a parable of dying and becoming. Winter dissolves into spring, summer dies into autumn and then winter again. Goethe suggests that when we observe these processes outside of ourselves we can begin to understand them within ourselves. This understanding can help us to find the courage to embrace dying and becoming.

One of the most poetic and miraculous examples of this process is the caterpillar's transformation from a creature that creeps along the earth into a winged butterfly. The caterpillar begins the process of dying and becoming by spinning itself a cocoon. Whilst within this dark, enclosed space, it dissolves completely and become a formless soup. Out of this soup, a new and entirely different creature begins to form. The butterfly begins to form in opposition to its old form. Still the process is not over. Once it has completed its metamorphosis, the butterfly must struggle to free itself from its cocoon. This resistance is not an unhappy misfortune; only by meeting and overcoming it can the butterfly gain its freedom and independence.

Goethe and Ibsen describe processes in the natural world in order for us to be able to see them in the human soul. There, dying and becoming are connected with the way that we meet our own challenges and our subsequent willingness to allow them to change us, to allow them to deepen us. What exactly does it mean to embrace dying and becoming? How does embracing it make it possible to feel that our life has cohesion and meaning? How does it help us feel at home on the earth?

In order to answer those questions I need to explore another important aspect of dying and becoming, which the poet John Keats called *negative capability*. He says:

At once it struck me what qualities went to form a man of achievement... I mean negative capability, that is when a man is capable of being able to be in uncertainties, mysteries, doubts, without any irritable reaching for facts and reason.[17]

The butterfly 'does' negative capability by instinct. We humans have to cultivate it. It is like moving house. We must die to what we were and leave our old 'home'. As it recedes from our sight, we find ourselves in a place which is neither where we came from nor where we are going. This place, where all past securities have faded away, and future ones are not yet in sight, is the realm of negative capability. Keats says that in order really to inhabit this place, we need to learn to be in uncertainty without any 'irritable reaching after facts and reason'. We can neither force solutions nor hurry the process in any way. Instead we must endure its very real discomfort until the future arises out of the process, rather than out of our wish to end our experience of uncertainty.

Keats understood just how challenging and painful being in a place of negative capability is. When we have lost what we know, and not yet found our new truth, we feel skinless and vulnerable. That vulnerability leaves us feeling anxious and uncertain, and those feelings leave us feeling exposed and humiliated. The caterpillar's body dissolves; for us, it is our inner certainties which dissolve – a kind of body of the soul. Everything that we have ever taken for granted recedes. Everything that we believe and live by must be re-examined before our new self can emerge. Strangely, practice does not make it any easier to embrace this process. No matter how many times we go through it, it always fills us with dread. Every time, we fear that this time we will not make it through; we fear that we will be overwhelmed by chaos and cast into oblivion.

These experiences are very much part of our everyday existence. Creativity always involves this process. For example, I have found subjects and ways of working in different fields that seem to help me express whatever I am after. After some time they begin to seem hollow and they cease to convince me. This emerging hollowness always becomes apparent through a feeling of anxiety or depression. Such feelings, when heeded calmly, are always the herald of growth, but at first they leave me feeling daunted. I have to give away what I have done before and remain with nothing. This emptiness, this loss of identity, is always frightening and I am tempted to keep what I have for fear of not finding my new and better artistic language. Only when I am prepared to face this fear and let go does the new work begin to arise.

We might wonder, if it is so painful, why anyone could ever embrace this process. For me, a better question might be: 'What is the cost of *not embracing* negative capability?' The philosopher John MacMurray[18] says, 'dogmatism is the mechanisation of the mind and conformity the mechanisation of the emotions.' Both conformity and dogmatism come about when we fear to live in movement which, as all life is lived in movement, means to fear life itself. Conformity and dogmatism are the complete opposite of what Ibsen, Goethe and Keats write about and encourage. Conformity and dogmatism attempt to find simple solutions that protect us from the need to change and grow, to think for ourselves and to develop and deepen. They are an attempt to construct a secure and predictable place from which to live our lives. If we live like this we may have a sense of certainty but our world becomes small and anything that challenges our point of view becomes a threat. This was the way that most of the adults had lived, in my childhood. Learning from those who had not and from the whole realm of literature, art and the history of ideas I began to explore ways of embracing intensity myself. Although this was a hard choice, one that meant failing and yet learning to endure, it also gave me a real, much-needed sense of meaning.

Chapter 10
The Conversation

My mother and I had been near-strangers for years. This distance was overcome when, at the age of fifty-four, she was diagnosed with leukaemia. Understanding the seriousness of her illness I tried to spend as much time with her as I could. On this occasion she was staying at my brother's house in London before being taken to hospital to undergo a so-called 'simple procedure'. I was sitting with her to keep her company before we set off to the hospital. My father was in another room reading while we talked. As well as suffering from leukaemia, she had lost her short-term memory, so our conversations at that time were quite often dislocated and repetitive.

Yet that morning, completely unexpectedly, something shifted. My mother stopped being vague. Instead she felt present and touchingly soft. The atmosphere in the room changed, and the air seemed full of new possibilities. She started to speak in a completely different way. Perhaps the seriousness of the situation and the vulnerability caused by her frail state of health allowed her momentarily to drop her guard, and let me see who she really was.

This conversation is probably the most beautiful thing that has ever happened to me. She looked at me very shyly. She told me that she knew that Freddie had been a bad man and she was very sorry for what had happened to me. She then went on to describe something of her own life.

She told me that she had been to Hornsey Art School when she was young. She had tried to make art but had found the challenge of making work far too frightening. So she decided to crush that part of herself, hoping that if she suppressed her creativity, it would stop causing her so much anxiety and pain. She wanted to avoid difficult feelings at all costs. Her strategy was to make sure she was never silent or unoccupied. This was why she kept the radio on; this was why she always needed a distraction. She was trying to drown out her inner voice and to hide from her feelings.

She then looked at me with heart-breaking openness and told me that I too had been a victim of her campaign of self-destruction. She said that from the moment I was born, she'd found my presence disquieting. Sharing many of her gifts, I had constantly reminded her of all that she would not own in herself. My very presence had been a source of pain. I looked very like my mother and even sounded like her. She had tried to kill and numb her own artistic nature but, whenever she looked at me, she saw the very self that she feared: the creative self that she wanted to starve of life and space. It had been terrible for her to have a daughter who was so passionately interested in art and literature. She had dismissed my enthusiasm, dismissed my success in winning prizes, and poured cold water on the encouragement of my teachers because of her fear of her own creativity. She acknowledged that my childhood must have been very hard, owning that she had done everything she could to destroy me. My creativity was a terrifying presence knocking at the door of her soul and reminding her of the creative self she had wanted to kill.

This last conversation, brought about through her illness, drew us together after years of distance. Throughout her life she had lived in a world which refused to acknowledge the existence of suffering and death; she had no-one in her life with whom she could discuss her difficult feelings. But now, in extremis, I was there to hear her and she shared her grief that she was dying. I didn't change the subject or try to cheer her up with false hope. I just listened.

Throughout this incredible conversation I remained completely silent. I dared not move, or utter a sound, for fear that I would break the spell and that she would stop speaking. Eventually my father came into the room and we left for the hospital. I had to go to an unrelated meeting nearby, so they dropped me off on the way. I got out of the car and leaned into her window to kiss her goodbye, but she still wanted to speak. While in Botton I had met my future husband, Tom. My mother had only met him once but now she asked me whether he loved me. I laughed and told her that he always says, "Darling Deb you make my life 3-D!" She told me she was so glad that I was not alone and we kissed each other goodbye. I looked straight into her eyes. She was soft, open, warm and concerned. I had never before experienced that kind of attention or love from her. She had become my mother.

We never saw each other again. The 'small procedure' was too much for her body to bear and she died. However, the last look that we exchanged was one of total acceptance. We had finally recognised and loved each other.

· · · · · · ·

When my mother acknowledged how awful Freddie had been, nearly twenty years after her initial denial of my experience, she released me from the unspoken sense that I was the problem. When she acknowledged that her fear of her own creativity had made her try to crush mine, she released me from the feeling that to care about art and literature, to explore ideas and try to live deeply, was 'too intense'. It was clear from her obvious remorse that she was very sorry that she had not helped and comforted me when I first told her about Freddie. It was also clear from her gratitude for the way we could speak together that, what had once been characterised as 'living my life as if it was a novel', or being 'too intense', was exactly what she needed as she faced her death.

I had always felt that my unhappy relationship with my mother meant that I must in some way be unlovable. In this conversation I learned, at least in theory, that this was not so.

As this new story unfolded I felt my whole history convulse and dissolve. Nothing I had ever thought or felt still applied. This was dying and becoming in practice, for me. And for my mother too. She was never at home in life, at home in her own skin. Her fear of manifesting her obvious gifts and abilities had made her restless and unable to bear stillness, and had even made her hurt me. Now she was physically dying. That she chose this moment to embrace the process of dying and becoming in her life of soul is the greatest gift she could have given me. She needn't have spoken to me in that way and I know it took a great deal of courage to do so. It meant facing things that hadn't been faced for years, and it meant owning up to them and expressing remorse. For years she had fought against who she really was, at the last moment it was her deepest self that was triumphant.

Just as she was leaving life, she became more than my anxious, restless mother. She was who she really was and became at home in life. It is never too late to learn to live with openness.

MacMurray[19] describes another aspect of what is possible when we choose to live with this kind of openness. Since I was different, I had become the enemy for my mother. When we choose to live in process, not only do we feel better in our skin but others cease to be the enemy, becoming instead part of 'the living, colourful multiplicity of difference'. This, he explains, can only be experienced if we dare to become spontaneous and give up our security in favour of 'the spirit of adventure'. Shakespeare was able to empathise with the whole world through his capacity to bear negative capability. He was able to appreciate 'the living, colourful, multiplicity of difference'. He was not constrained by conformity and dogmatism. This is the reward of the dying and becoming of negative capability. It may be demanding and painful to pass through the experience of vulnerability and its accompanying feeling of humiliation, but those experiences are only a stage upon the way. It is a hard way but it is a way which leads to abundance and a capacity to grow beyond the narrow walls of ourselves into the wide vistas of life in all its variety.

Chapter 11
Embracing Vulnerability

I f we are to die and become, if we are to live our lives more intensely, as the Button Moulder told Peer Gynt, as my mother did in her last moments, then this means giving up our security and allowing ourselves to become completely vulnerable. We will need to bear contradictions and tolerate the place where there are only questions, where answers have not yet emerged. We die, we enter the realm of negative capability and then we endure. Only when we let go and endure does our new self emerge. This new self cannot be rushed and it cannot be forced. It only emerges when the time is ripe. For my mother, it only emerged as she knew she was dying.

I did not have to wait that long, but I still needed a long and sometimes painful period of digesting, firstly to heal the damage I had experienced as a child and secondly, to understand and grow from the loss of community life. As time went on I was to discover that my childhood and what had happened in Botton were deeply connected.

When I left Botton I was in deep crisis. I had lost what I lived for; I had lost the work that gave my life meaning, and I had lost my status as a well-loved teacher and co-worker. Strangely it was this crisis that served me, that helped me understand just how difficult it is to be authentic and to remain true to oneself. Peer Gynt is all of us and our own life and struggle brings his struggle out of the realm of ideas into visceral reality. When my relationships broke down in Botton, life became so painful and disordered it seemed impossible to make meaning out of the chaos. I felt ashamed and humiliated, and I decided to try to forget my entire past. Instead of staying with the pain, instead of staying in negative capability, I became driven. When I had worked in Botton I had worked because I cared for what we were doing. Now I worked to make myself feel better, to rid myself of the shame of being such a loser. I hoped that by building a new and successful life I would redeem the past, regain my status and forget those sad times.

None of those attempts succeeded and, instead of lifting myself out of my morass, I sunk deeper and deeper into it. Only in the depths of my despair did I finally realise that I needed to let go of the idea that I could avoid the consequences of my loss. I saw that I had to allow the reality of my new existence as a failure to take up its central place in my inner life. I had to die to my old self in order to begin the long and painful journey to my new self. In order to do this I needed to enter the frightening space of negative capability. Only then would I find the right orientation to take hold of my experience and try to understand it. I saw that in order to reach that place of understanding I would have to ask what my part in it all had been. This was the most frightening part of the process but I knew that only then would I be able to grow from all that had happened.

To mark my decision I performed a kind of ritual. I went into the sitting room of the house in Middlesbrough that I had moved to after leaving Botton, and I sat down on the sofa. I then leaned back into the cushions so that I felt physically supported. I felt very frightened but I also was determined to face myself in a new way. I addressed a great unknown. In my mind's eye I imagined that there was a guardian of my life, a kind of accompanying angel. I told this being and myself that no matter how painful or frightening it was, I wanted truly to know what had happened to cause the breakdown at Botton, even if it meant finding out that I was responsible. I found myself stretching out my arms and opening them. I wanted to embrace and own my new, bleak future as a failure. As I embraced it, I stopped thinking about how I could hurry myself out of this state. Instead I accepted that it would probably take me years to work through the failure of my deepest ideals. Strangely, although this didn't take away my problems, it did give me a new acceptance of them. I was no longer struggling. I was living in the here and now.

Up until that point, no matter what had happened to me, I had always had a sense that life was meaningful. I was also convinced that, no matter what, I had a future. My early memory of the huge space behind my head had left me feeling connected to a deeper reality and that gave my life a certain sweetness, regardless of what else was going on. Now everything had changed. I had lost this fundamental belief in the value of my existence. I lay in my bed in Middlesbrough and suffered a panic attack as I realised that my previous confidence that life had meaning and purpose had simply dissolved.

In my imagination, I looked out into the vast reaches of that previously welcoming space and saw not the realm from which I had come as a child but, rather, something overwhelmingly huge that now seemed to mock me with its indifference. I felt physically sick and overwhelmed by dread as the last vestiges of the foundations of my existence fell away, casting me adrift in a great sea of blank and vacant space. This new and dreadful confrontation with indifference and nothingness entered me like a cold, wounding blade.

Strangely, as it penetrated me, something in me shifted. A new, completely independent part of me emerged and found its voice. I acknowledged that I no longer had that sense of meaning and I accepted this frightening new reality as part of my life. But I did not feel defeated. Instead I accessed a new energy and I found myself deciding to live as if it still mattered how I behaved, despite the loss of my old certainties. I was determined not to let my disappointment make me become hard and cynical, or timid and uninvolved. Trying to live decently was no longer dependent on the success of any project or relationship; it arose instead out of a free decision. I willed myself to work and to keep going. I sensed that to do this was to make my own meaning despite my confrontation with its frightening loss.

Although life was hard, once I was in that state of acceptance I found not only pain, but also new inner resources. I found myself thinking of a long forgotten image. It was Grunewald's painting of the Resurrection of Christ. This painting is part of the altar of the Monastery of St Antony in Isenheim, where the monks had created a hospital for people suffering from disease. It is now displayed in Colmar in France. This image had had a huge impact on me when I first saw it. I was twenty-one years old and newly arrived at Botton from university. As I looked at the sun-like radiance of the resurrected Christ I realised that I had to think of the Christian story in a very different way. Instead of it being limited to conventional religion, this image of Christ represented something universal, far beyond what was contained either by the name Christianity or the Church. I realised that what the picture actually represented was the universal human capacity to unfold our potential in all its radiance.

Now, as I remembered that image, I remembered too that it was part of a much larger work, and that it represented the end of a process and not the beginning. Before the radiant image of the resurrection, there was an image of a terrible and humiliating death, an image of the Crucifixion. In this ancient world, this form of execution was more than painful. Its horror lay not only in pain but in the fact that the naked body of the criminal was being exposed to contempt. I connected the story of the Crucifixion with the universal concept of dying and becoming. I remembered the caterpillar and the butterfly and I began to think of my pain and dishonour, my failure, in a different way. I wondered if it were not an end but an ongoing part of a much bigger process. I suspected that the pain I was experiencing might indeed be the close of my old life, but that if I could bear it and resist the temptation to escape it or numb it out, I could grow beyond loss and emptiness to a new future, to my own resurrection. The Christian story moved out of history and came alive in my own dying and becoming, my own capacity to endure and overcome. Life did not stop being hard but I began to live with regeneration as well as pain.

When I first left Botton I was so depressed that, not being able to concentrate, I found myself unable to read. As I began to find myself again, I also recovered my ability to focus and the first book I picked up was Vera Brittain's autobiography, *Testament of Youth*[20]. This book and its sequels had a profound impact on how I was able to understand my own situation. Vera Brittain's life encompassed both World Wars. She had just been awarded a place at university as the First World War was declared. Universities had only just been opened to women. They could attend classes but they were still not awarded degrees. Just as her independent life was about to begin, the war confronted her with a new choice. Driven by youthful idealism, and despite her huge struggle to get to Cambridge, she sacrificed her hard-won prize so that she could join the war effort. She became a nurse. Her fiancé and brother became soldiers. By the end of the war everyone she loved had died and, apart from her terrible personal loss, it had become clear to her that the war had not been the noble endeavour they had been led to believe. Instead it had been a waste of the lives of millions of young people.

Her whole generation was left feeling betrayed. Their innocence and their naïvety had been exploited. That so many had been lost for a lie left Brittain profoundly depressed. Her pain was exacerbated by not being able to speak to anyone about her feelings. Addressing the wasteful horror of the war was too painful for most people. It would have meant facing the fact that all those whom they had lost had died for no reason. Horror of that awful truth kept the truth at bay. What is more, anyone who dared to speak the truth was made to feel like a pariah, or even demonised.

Brittain tried to speak but was met with cold dismissal or outright aggression; this left her teetering on the edge of madness. When she looked into the mirror she began to see, looking back at her, not her own countenance, but rather an ugly, witch-like face.

As I had learned from my mother's relationship with me, when we are unable to bear looking at a painful truth, anyone bringing it up and asking us to look at it becomes monstrous. The witch-like face she saw was the projection of those who had cast her in the role of monster. She had internalised their terror and begun to believe in those projections.

Fortunately, Vera Brittain became friends with a young woman, Winifred Holtby, who was able to hear her story without flinching. Being heard in turn enabled Vera Brittain to write *Testament of Youth*. Telling her story enabled her to find her inner orientation and to begin the process of her own healing. This book was, in fact, much more than her personal story. By her writing it so honestly and authentically, she lifted her story into the realm of the universal and gave her generation a voice.

Despite the betrayal of her generation, Vera Brittain did not give up her youthful ideals. Instead, they were tempered by pain and experience and she went on to become a passionate campaigner for peace for the rest of her life. During the Second World War she continued to campaign and she stayed in London writing her *Peace Letters*, protesting against the blanket bombing of civilians in Germany. Once again she was not heard. Instead she was seen as a traitor. Even that did not deter her. After the war she took the unpopular stand of fundraising to help feed the dispossessed civilians of Germany as well as the rest of war-torn Europe. The pain that resulted from her disillusionment about the First World War could have made Vera Brittain give up being involved in any kind of social activism or idealism. She could have withdrawn from public life and lived just for herself. She chose instead to transform her naïve idealism into practical wisdom and to continue to work for a better world.

This story became my guide book for coping with my own life. It contained a template for understanding my own story. In community I too had given myself away to something because of my idealism. Our unresolved conflict had left me feeling betrayed by older people whom I had trusted to know best. When I tried to speak about those difficult times, in an attempt to understand them, I too was silenced. Like her, I too had internalised that rejection of my need to speak so that I was left feeling dangerous and unwelcome.

Her story helped me see my own with a new objectivity. I understood that to be young and unguarded is part of life and that failure is something that no one can escape. I saw that the issue is not that we fail but rather how we deal with it, what it calls up in us as new qualities and character, what it gives us in the way of insights. My story was happening on a much smaller scale, but in recognising its universality I was able to stop feeling so alone, isolated and so particularly stupid and foolish. Instead I felt I was walking a path that many had walked before me, and many would walk long after I was gone. I saw that I was normal and that, instead of feeling cast out of the human family, I understood that what had happened to me was very much part of being human.

Chapter 12
Love and Power

When my mother told me the history of her own discomfort with creativity, and her subsequent squashing of mine, she was also giving me back my own history. I now understood where my lack of confidence in applying to art school had come from and I understood how I had coped with my uncreative state. Like many blocked artists I had dealt with my blocks by finding a way to be near the thing I loved. I did not practise art but I looked at it, gave lectures about it and encouraged others to make it. Freed from the laming effect of her discouragement, I now began to believe I could overcome that lack of confidence and study art for myself. So when I heard about Leith School of Art, an inspirational new school in Edinburgh, I applied and was offered a place for the following September.

Meanwhile Tom had completed his training as a priest in his church, The Christian Community. Whilst I was waiting to start, I joined Tom in his first posting in Marburg in Germany. I went there to prepare for our marriage and for my entry into art school. The church and our flat were in a Renaissance building called the *Hochzeithaus*, which means marriage house. We lived adjacent to a small market square where there were regular farmers' markets selling food and flowers. It was so beautiful I would wake up in the morning and look out of my window and just begin to laugh.

We married in Germany, and not long after our wedding we returned to Britain. I began my five year training and I made

91

new friends. I was embarking on a new life learning something I really cared about, and I was living with someone I loved. This gave me a new sense of being home. Paradoxically, this happiness and security gave me the confidence to start therapy, for help with understanding my early childhood wounds.

During my short stay in Germany I had been given a postcard by a new friend. On it was an image of an installation by Joseph Beuys called *Show Your Wound*. This statement filled me with excitement. He said about this work:

> *And when I say "Show it! Show the wound that we have inflicted upon ourselves during the course of our development", it is because the only way to progress and become aware of it is to show it.*[21]

This image seemed to contain the essence of something I needed to understand. Later, when I actually studied Beuys and his widened concept of art, it became a catalyst for new work whilst his ideas became the means of artistic expression of my deepest questions. Meanwhile, I embarked on finding a way to live with both my sadness and my new-found happiness and to give them both equal attention.

When I first left Botton, many of my old friends from university visited me. They had all made much more conventional choices than me and had careers in law, management, medicine and so on. I expected that their lives would have gone smoothly and that they would be radiating confidence and success, unlike me. I assumed that my problems had been caused by the fact that, since I did not live in the mainstream, we did not have proper structures in place to cope with our problems. I was quite wrong. Despite coming from very structured work environments, my friends too were suffering from unresolved conflicts. I was beginning to discover that conflict was a universal issue, regardless of the aims and intentions of the people involved. In his *Letters to a Young*

Poet[22], Rilke advises us to learn to love our questions and to wait until they are ready to reveal their answers. He says that we need to develop patience because this can sometimes take a very long time.

Many years after I first formulated my questions about human beings' capacity to live their ideals, I met Adam Kahane[23].

Adam is one of the founder members of Reos Partners. He works in some of the most challenging places in the world, facilitating dialogue and transformation. I first met him when he delivered a lecture entitled 'Striding into the Sea: Five Steps to Addressing Tough Social Challenge'. He described the tools that he had developed to analyse the problems that we all face, living and working together. It was a lecture that had a profound impact on me: through hearing him speak I was finally able to diagnose and understand the process of disintegration I had experienced in Botton and to understand my role in it.

He began his lecture with the following words:

> For the past fifteen years I have focused my attention on answering one question: how can we address our toughest social challenges? Our two most common ways of dealing with these challenges are the extreme ones, war and peace. Either we push through what we want regardless of what others want – but inevitably people push back. Or we try not to push anything or anyone – but that just leaves the situation as it is. Neither of these things work; we need a better way: a way beyond war and peace.

He went on to explore the concepts of power and love. Quoting the theologian Paul Tillich he explained that power is 'the drive of everything living to realise itself with increasing intensity and extensity'[24]. Love, on the other hand is 'the drive towards the unity of the separated.' In Adam's words, "power in this sense is the drive to achieve one's purpose, to get one's job done, to grow.

Love, on the other hand, is 'the drive to reconnect that which is whole, which is one, which is fragmented." Adam went on to explain that if we want to be able to understand and address tough social challenges, then we need to be able to recognise and work with these two poles, with both love and power. They are in fact interdependent: each has both a generative and a degenerate face, and the degenerate face of both of them arises out of the lack of the other. In other words, when power is not mitigated by love it becomes degenerate power. It becomes, in Adam's words, tyrannical, abusive and even genocidal. When love is not strengthened by power it becomes degenerate and ineffective. Building his thesis, he added:

> Our power becomes degenerate when, because we are afraid of being hurt, we cut off our connection. Our love becomes degenerate when, because we are afraid of allowing or contributing to others being hurt, we cut off action. Our fears hold us back from being able to address our toughest challenges.

Overcoming the fear of being hurt or hurting others is crucial. This means learning to be honest about what is happening with others and learning to be vulnerable ourselves, without either being destructive. As he says, the choice is not between causing damage and doing nothing. The choice is to enter the process and find the language for meeting ourselves and each other in this vulnerable place of potential. Adam went on to quote Paul Tillich's most famous student, the American civil rights activist Martin Luther King Jr. In one of his last speeches, King spoke of the imperative of reconciling power and love. He said, "Power without love is reckless and abusive; love without power is sentimental and anaemic. This collision of immoral power with powerless morality constitutes the major crisis of our time."[25]

To illustrate the different faces of love and power more

concretely Adam then spoke about a conversation with the Italian feminist Paula Melchiori:

> *She pointed out to me that we can see these two sets of faces clearly if we look at stereotyped gender roles. The father embodying masculine power goes out to work. The generative face of his power is that he can create something valuable in the world. The degenerative face of his power is that he can become so focused on his work that he forgets about his connection to other people, and becomes a robot or a tyrant. By contrast the mother, embodying feminine love, stays at home to raise the children. The generative face of her love is that she literally gives life to her child. The degenerative face of her love is that she can become so protective of the child she forgets about its need for self-realisation and so stunts its growth.*

Adam then shared the observation of family systems therapist, Edwin Friedman, who had noticed that if one were to look at the root of every toxic social group, small or large, it would be possible to identify someone who takes up the role of what he called 'peace-monger'. The term peace-monger contrasts with that of the peace-maker. The word peace-maker has very positive connotations because peace-makers resolve conflict. Peace-mongers, on the other hand, do not resolve conflict; they suppress or bypass it. They avoid acknowledging and tackling problems and they discourage others from doing the same. By avoiding conflict, they appear to foster peace. What they are actually doing is making a kind of pseudo-peace. Such peace is not built on any real resolution and so it inevitably fails. The peace-monger chooses this option because, in their deepest heart, they believe that the risks and hard work associated with really acknowledging and working through struggle are so dangerous and overwhelming that compromise is all we can really hope for. Fear lies at the root of both degenerate power and love. The role of the peace-monger is also governed by fear. Not only does peace-mongering prevent the possibility of real resolution, it is also responsible for the continuance of the status quo. If the status quo is harmful, a situation like bullying for example, the peace-monger is not creating harmony as they believe; rather they are colluding with what needs facing up to and transforming.

The insights of the writer and psychologist M Scott Peck add to this picture.[26] Scott Peck has researched community dynamics both in his books and in his organisation, the Foundation for Community Encouragement. He highlights the difference between what he called *pseudo-community* and its direct counterpart, *authentic* or _real_ *community*. We can experience pseudo-community in any group that has not yet faced and worked through its challenges. In such a community people appear to be in harmony, but this is only because difficulties have not been raised and confronted. As soon as the group faces a challenge, pseudo-community disintegrates. The group then enters what Scott Peck calls the wilderness. At the point of disintegration the group may panic and want to return to pseudo-community. This is a sensitive moment because it contains the potential for transformation or failure. It is an experience of dying and becoming in a community sense. The wilderness, with all its associated discomfort and anxiety, is a form of negative capability. Scott Peck says of this state of wilderness that it is important that the members of the group not only bear their fear and discomfort but also commit to staying in the group. In so doing the group will move from pseudo-community to wilderness to authentic community. This is a risk that the peace-monger is not able to bear. The potential for failure and for chaos is just too frightening. They are therefore prepared to settle for a grey compromise that lacks the life and abundance of true community. Ironically, if these compromises are made over and over again, the group will become ever more toxic so that, when their problems are finally exposed, they will be far more complex and demand much more courage and effort to work through.

At the end of his lecture, in conversation with the audience, Adam also noted with some surprise that the worst kinds of behaviour that he had encountered when working with groups had not been in large corporate settings, as he would have expected, but rather in consciously idealistic organisations. He suspected that idealistic groups were uncomfortable with the whole issue of power, which then remained unnamed and unacknowledged. Ignoring the existence of power and its role does not mean that it is not there. Rather it is there, but in insidious ways. With no transparency and therefore no accountability, such power structures gain an unseen foothold in the community and inevitably become degenerate and therefore abusive and tyrannical.

Adam works internationally with very serious world issues but his thesis can be applied to much more modest situations. Using his analysis, I found myself able to describe our experience of community breakdown.

At Botton, Peter did not believe that it was necessary to create formal structures to ensure that the long-term co-workers were aware of the aims and intentions of the community. As a consequence, there were no structures in place to hold us all accountable to this purpose. I believe that Peter chose to work in this way because, despite his many gifts, he was seriously uncomfortable when faced with conflict. He often played the role of peace-monger and abnegated his own power. He believed that if he loved someone enough they would eventually support his aims. As time went on, and conflict after conflict was smoothed over or avoided, the community began to suffer. Transparency and clarity of purpose were sacrificed for what became not authentic community but the pseudo-community described by Scott Peck. To make the transition from pseudo-community to authentic community, we would have needed to be a group of strong individuals with the resilience to bear the 'wilderness' that would have resulted from facing our problems and not smoothing them away. We were not.

At Botton, we often talked of selflessness. We wanted to be unselfish and work for the wider aims of the community. As I listened to Adam's lecture, I understood that in fact we had not been developing our capacity to be unselfish. Instead, we had given away our own agency in the name of being tolerant and keeping the peace. We too had become peace-mongers. Adam speaks of the need to become literate in both love and power. By not understanding the power pole, we had failed to become individuals. Only individuals have the capacity to be really unselfish because only a person with a strong identity has something to give away. Without power, without self-realisation, our love had become sentimental, anaemic and powerless. When conflict could no longer be contained, the battle became very ugly. The culture of self-abnegation and the denial of power had created a culture in which the most painful struggles and rejections could, and did, occur.

Realising that I had not developed a strong self brought a great sense of liberation. I had known community at its most positive and creative, and I had known it at its most calamitous. I was broken-hearted to leave Botton, but now I realised that the failure of my community life had just as much potential and significance as its success. I saw that without that conflict and what seemed at first like exile, I would not have awoken to my own power. I would not have become myself. Finally understanding what had happened in Botton meant that I could move on. Adam's lecture had set me free. It had also reignited my hope for future community building.

Chapter 13
Truth and Reconciliation

Adam's work on the international stage helped me understand my own experiences of conflict. At around that time, I was also reading Desmond Tutu's record of the reconciliation process in South Africa. This was to help me with another unresolved aspect of my personal story. Post-apartheid, the South African government of National Unity established what became known as the Truth and Reconciliation Commission. The aims of the Commission were to help South Africans to find a morally acceptable way of coming to terms with their past and to foster reconciliation. I used what I learned from that extraordinary process to understand my more ordinary family situation.

The work of the Commission was documented in a book written by Desmond Tutu called *No Future without Forgiveness*[27]. To set the scene for his book, Tutu refers to a play called *Death and the Maiden* by the Chilean author Ariel Dorman[28]. The heroine of the play is a victim of torture at the hands of the forces of General Pinochet. After Pinochet was toppled, a blanket amnesty was declared for all the perpetrators of violence during the coup, so it was possible to find oneself sitting on the bus beside one's torturer. In the play, the heroine meets her torturer by chance. She needs him to acknowledge what he has done to her, so she overpowers him in order to elicit a confession. She asks him over and over again if he was the man who tortured her, which he repeatedly denies. Driven by despair, she threatens him with a gun and he finally acknowledges his guilt. Strangely, as soon as she hears the truth, she is able to let him go. She does not need revenge, she needs truth.

Tutu explains this in the following words:

> *His denial hit at the core of her being, at her integrity, at her identity and these things were all tied up intimately with her experiences, with her memory. Denial subverted her personhood; she was in a real sense her memory.*

This process, as described by Tutu, helped me to understand the depression that descended on me shortly after my mother's confession. Tutu says that being lied to subverts one's personhood. He explains how our sense of self is connected to our memories of what has happened to us. All my memories were masked and hidden behind stories that overwrote my own. I had spent a large part of the first ten years of my life living with a man who abused and intimidated me, and who told me that if I told the truth I would die. I had been led to believe that this man was my father. I had then spent the rest of my childhood and young adulthood feeling completely unwelcome in my family. My mother's irritation and discouragement had left me feeling that I could never get it right. Finally, on the brink of her death, my mother had told me the truth: the problem between us had its roots in her own struggles, not in my shortcomings and flaws.

Why then was I so depressed when I had been told the truth? Slowly I began to understand. I had not been really able to have any feelings about my early childhood, despite my childhood decision to 'feel my feelings'. I truly believed that I had survived it. I had endured and kept going. I had often said to myself as a little girl, "Don't cry, it is not safe." I now saw that mere survival is a strategy that only works for a time. Although I was trying to stay connected with my feelings in an attempt not to repeat the behaviour of the rest of my family, I was completely disconnected from the feelings I had had when living with Freddie, not because of a conscious act of denial, but because I was too busy surviving to stop and feel. If we do not face and deal with our legitimate pain it doesn't go away. It simply surfaces as illegitimate pain or neurosis. This is what happened to me after I learned the truth during the final, revealing conversation with my mother: what I hadn't felt consciously appeared in the form of depression.

These deep, unexpressed feelings and my failure to speak up in Botton were closely linked. One of the things that our parents can and should give us is self-belief. I had not been offered that gift. I then went on to work in idealistic settings, where the whole idea of developing a strong identity was confused with being self-seeking and selfish. I lacked a sense of self, and therefore the healthy confidence to discriminate and trust my judgment. Instead, at Botton, I fell too easily into the role of the abused child, doing anything in order to be accepted by the authority figures in my life. Peter and his fellow founders had become my new parents, and my relationship pattern with such figures remained dysfunctional.

• • • • • • •

Helen Keller was born blind and deaf, which left her isolated from the world. In her autobiography, she describes her frustration at not being able to communicate with other human beings[29]. This all changed when, after many attempts at transmitting language, her teacher held her hand under a tap and inscribed the word 'water' onto her palm. As she felt the water and the letters spelling water, she understood the movements on her hand were describing the substance flowing over her hand. She was at last able to connect with the means by which she could communicate with the world.

Adam Kahane and Desmond Tutu were my equivalent of the water and the touch of Helen's teacher. Learning about power and love and the Commission for Truth and Reconciliation gave me tools to understand the past I had spent years trying to unravel. In the words of the Button Moulder I had not given in to incomprehension. It was no easy task.

This long period of questioning was of great concern for some of my family and former colleagues. Some were embarrassed by me and others worried about me. They wanted me to forget it all and cheer up. Often I was made to feel that I was too sensitive or incapable of moving on. I was, on one level, what mainstream culture most discourages: vulnerable, benighted, one of life's losers. I hated feeling like that but I did so for many years. Nevertheless I kept on. Perhaps I was able to remain in that vulnerable state because of that early decision as a child to feel my feelings no matter what.

It is very hard to do the work of trying to understand one's life. What is clear to me, however, is that if I hadn't stayed with those feelings, if I hadn't kept trying to find answers no matter how exposed I felt, I might have saved face but I would not have found myself. That alchemical moment of meeting the ideas I needed, and seeing their connection to my own situation was like germination. I was dealing with something that seemed incomprehensible. With the tools of Kahane and Tutu's insights I was able to unravel the muddle and find out both what had happened, and what had been my part in it. I no longer felt blind and deaf as I had before. Instead I was able to diagnose, judge and discriminate. I tremble at the thought that I could have missed that opportunity by being too proud to be broken and lost. If I had contained my feelings and numbed them out I would not have found the ideas I needed: ideas that would reaffirm my conviction that it is worth trying to work with idealism and trying to work with other people. Failing and failing again leads to growth and failing again better.

Chapter 14
Questioning the Good Life

What was it about my sadness that made people so uncomfortable? We live in the so-called free world. That world is dominated by the mass media and the advertising industry which paints a picture of the good life, a life described by Rilke in the *Duino Elegies* as the Land of Pain: the kind of life where we try to keep everything difficult at bay. It promises us freedom, but this is reduced to the freedom to make money; fulfilment comes through our consuming and indulging our every whim. The myth of the 'good life' only makes sense if we are happy. To keep us happy we are offered every distraction imaginable. We must be distracted from our inner lives, our sadness, our questions, our fears and anxieties: anything that will awaken our capacity to find out who we are and what we really want.

Of course, modern democracy has far more noble roots than the myth of the 'good life'. Perhaps we can reclaim the deep story of democracy and wrest it back from the insidious influence of superficiality. For hundreds of years, people have struggled for a better world in order that we might be protected from every kind of tyranny, that we might be free, that we might be happy. The American Declaration of Independence was an expression of that struggle. It asserts these rights. But freedom in this sense was not the freedom to do and have what we like. Rather it is a call to self-realisation and responsibility. It is a call to become the master of one's own soul.

In the same way, happiness does not mean the anaesthetised

existence which is the siren song of the 'good life'. Happiness in this context refers rather to the joy of being able to manifest our potential and to put that potential at the service of something greater than ourselves. This means more than simply working for money and the pursuit of leisure; it means to find and live one's vocation. Frederik Buechner describes vocation as the place where 'your deep gladness meets the world's need.'[30] For me, as for Buechner, this is what it means to be happy.

Peer Gynt was going to be melted down for buttons because he had not lived intensely, because he had given in to incomprehension. To live intensely means to go against the grain of contemporary culture and live as if what we do, what we think and how we behave *does* matter, not only for our self-becoming but for the future of our world community. In order to do that, we have to begin with the stuff of our lives, with what happens to us. We have to give this stuff, our experiences, the attention they deserve, to feel and digest them and to find their meaning. This is not possible if we are constantly being encouraged to cheer up and be happy, and to forget and smooth over the things that have challenged us. Rilke wrote, again in the *Duino Elegies,* that to regret being sad is to become a waster of sorrows. For him sadness was like winter. Without winter, nature could not gather the fruits of summer; without winter, it could not prepare for spring. Without sadness we cannot understand the past and become the growing human being who points to the future.

The process of dying and becoming, the experience of negative capability cannot happen without being vulnerable.

Vulnerability is also important in our relationships to others. If we are able to embrace all of our inner lives, both 'good' and 'bad', then the need to have secrets from ourselves or from others diminishes. Strength comes from facing what we fear rather than fleeing from it, from revealing what we fear rather than hiding it. If relationships are built on this basis, they have strength; a strength based on being known in our weakness and our capacities and yet still loved, perhaps even loved more. With this comes a deeper intimacy and energy and a possibility to build trusting alliances. With such alliances comes the strength to do things in the world.

In her essay called *Women and Honor, Notes on Lying*[31], Adrienne Rich describes in her own way what I had met as a child, most specifically with my mother. I had seen the people around me numbing out their inner lives, and I had experienced how this blunted their capacity to feel engaged in life and to experience true intimacy. Rich's concern in this essay is what becomes possible when we create a culture where we can be open with each other about what is actually happening. She writes:

> *The possibilities that exist between two people, or among a group of people, are a kind of alchemy. They are the most interesting thing in life. The liar is someone who loses sight of these possibilities ... When someone tells me a piece of truth which has been withheld from me, and which I need to see my life more clearly, it may bring acute pain, but it can flood me with a sea-sharp wash of relief ... and extend the possibilities of truth between us.*

Keats also spoke of the role of suffering. He rejected the view of conventional religion that described the world as 'a vale of tears' from which we would be released by the arbitrary actions of God and the reward of heaven. He says instead that life is 'a vale of soul-making'. He wrote, 'I say 'Soul-making'. Soul as distinguished from an Intelligence – there may be intelligences or sparks of the divinity in millions – but they are not Souls till they acquire identities, till each one is personally itself.'[32] He then goes on to describe how to achieve this selfhood or, in his words, this 'Spirit creation'. He says, 'Do you not see how necessary a World of Pains and troubles is to school an Intelligence and make it a Soul? A Place where the heart must feel and suffer in a thousand diverse ways!' He was describing something not so different from Rilke's

Land of Pain. Both advocate the embracing of the whole of life, including its sufferings and the inevitability of death. For them, this was nothing to flee from or regret. On the contrary, the world with all its trials and sorrows was the perfect element, exactly what we needed to become our utterly unique selves.

Why does it matter that we become selves? Is it something we need to do just for our own personal happiness or does it have a wider relevance? In his book, *The Morals of Jesus*[33], Nicholas Peter Harvey quotes the anthropologist and writer Ernest Becker who says, 'It is the normal average men who like locusts have laid waste to the world in order to forget themselves.' If forgetting ourselves, avoiding our void, truly lays waste the world then it is not a neutral decision. Our actions will always have consequences. In the words of Becker, 'Someone has to pay'. The young heroine of *Where Angels Fear to Tread* says, 'There is never any knowing which of our actions, which of our idlenesses won't have things hanging on them forever.'[34] We need to become selves not only to fulfil our own potential: we need to become selves because we will have an impact on our families, our friends, our communities and our institutions. Everything that happens in the world begins with the actions of single people. By working on the work of art which is our life we work on the work of art which is our world.

Chapter 15
Auschwitz

On the sixtieth anniversary of the liberation of Auschwitz I was invited to give a lecture to commemorate those who had suffered there. I had first learned about the history of Germany's traumatic past at the age of eleven when I had found Leon Uris' book *Exodus*[35], which explores the fate of Jews in the twentieth century, lying around in our house. I read it all through the night, not putting it down until I had finished it late into the following morning. It was my first encounter with the *Shoah*. When I think of that night reading, I see it as the moment that I stopped being a child. The story of the Holocaust became a key theme in my life. The writer and poet Anne Michaels said she wrote about the Holocaust in her novels because she saw it as the story of her time. I agree with her. It is this story, with its millions of individual biographies, which shows me most clearly why it matters that we do the work of becoming a self; not just for ourselves but for the world.

Not long ago I was working in the city of Hamburg. Throughout the city, set into the pavements in front of houses and apartment blocks, are bronze cobblestones called 'stumbling stones'. On the stones, the names of the former Jewish inhabitants of the buildings are inscribed, with their birthdate, date of deportation and death date, if this is known. The stones are there not only to remind the population of Hamburg of those who were murdered but also to remind them that this crime was committed not in secret, but in the full light of day. At the time, ordinary citizens took advantage of the deportations, attending the street auctions of their neighbours' possessions. This says something of our capacity to be part of what Becker called 'laying waste the world'.

•••••••

In her book *Into That Darkness*[36], Gitta Sereny documents the journey of Franz Stangl from master weaver in a small town in Austria to Commandant of Treblinka, the death camp in Poland. Sereny tells how Stangl's fall into darkness began with a tiny act of discourtesy and self-deception. He had come from an unstable, poor background, and he longed for security and the status of a uniform. He decided to abandon his job as a weaver and apply to the police force without telling his boss. This small deception placed him on his first step on the path to running a death camp.

At the time Stangl became a policeman, the Nazi party was illegal in Austria, which meant he was sometimes present when Nazis were arrested and detained. When the Nazis eventually invaded Austria, he arranged with a fellow policeman to remove their names from anti-Nazi actions (another lie). As a result of his clean record, he was seen as potential Nazi material and was recruited into the Nazi party. He was then asked to sign a form saying he was willing to ignore his religious beliefs. He took this step without first discussing it with his wife. He was recruited to police the Euthanasia Project.

When asked by Sereny why he never questioned the murder of disabled adults and children, he said that, as the decision to conduct these killings was taken by highly trained doctors and scientists, he assumed that they knew better than him what it meant to act morally. He went on to be recruited to work on the Final Solution: the extermination of the Jews. Eventually, when he was asked to take over the organisation of Sobibor and then Treblinka he tried to say no. The response to his refusal was so threatening that he capitulated and became the commandant of those fearful places. It is estimated that 900,000 people were gassed and cremated in Treblinka. When this awful 'work' was completed, the Nazis dismantled the camp and built a farmhouse on the site to hide what had happened there. It is now a monument to the dead.

After the war, Stangl escaped via Rome to Argentina where he lived under his real name for twenty years. He was finally discovered and brought back to be tried in Germany. While serving his sentence, he agreed to be interviewed by Sereny. Throughout the interviews he refused to acknowledge any responsibility for anything that had happened. However, there was a moment in his last conversation with Sereny in which he allowed himself to admit that he had saved his own life at too great a cost. He said that he had come to feel that the burden of what he carried was so heavy that death would have been preferable. Sereny felt that this admission brought Stangl some sense of relief and healing. Nineteen hours after their conversation he died of heart failure. Sereny writes, 'I think he died because he had finally, however briefly, faced himself and told the truth; it was a monumental effort to reach that fleeting moment when he became the man he should have been.'[37]

The story of Stangl's loss of himself began with one small decision. He ignored his conscience and applied for a job without speaking about his intentions to his boss. From then on he was on the path which led from small deception to small deception into truly evil situations.

• • • • • • •

The commandant of Auschwitz, Rudolf Höss, was captured a year after the war and was tried both in Nuremberg and Poland. During his imprisonment in Poland he wrote his autobiography[38]. In his early years in the SS, he had worked in Dachau concentration camp. This camp, which was the first of its kind, was built just outside Munich to house political prisoners. Part of the SS ethos was the cultivation of ruthless hardness. In his autobiography, Höss describes how sickened he felt by the violence and suffering he saw in the camp. In his heart of hearts he had wanted to be a farmer but, afraid of the humiliation of not coming up to scratch, of being seen as soft and vulnerable, he ignored his feelings and schooled himself to endure what he naturally found unendurable. This decision unmade him: he too became a heartless instrument of the state and went on to oversee the monstrous death machine of Auschwitz. While he was in Poland he and his wife and children lived in a comfortable villa on the outskirts of the camp. His daughter later wrote about having enjoyed a 'beautiful childhood'.[39]

When I visited Auschwitz and walked up to the first camp, I had imagined that all that pain would leave a visible mark that singled it out as a place that was far beyond normal. I was wrong. The first camp was established in former barracks and is brick-built and almost pretty, with its poplar-lined paths and old-fashioned buildings. When Helen Arendt attended the trial of Adolf Eichmann she met someone so ordinary, so without personality, that she coined the phrase 'the banality of evil'. It is Peer Gynt's mediocrity that means that the Button Moulder comes to melt him down. It is this nothingness, this lack of selfhood, which made these men so vulnerable to manipulation and in every case this nothingness had its source in an unwillingness to face their feelings, and the questions that arise from those feelings.

The more I learned about Germany at the time of the Nazis the less able I was to see it as a German problem. I read story after story of what appeared to be trivial acts of human laziness or self-deception, but which led people into situations in which they became part of terrible and incomprehensible acts. Since those acts had their root in behaviours and decisions that were entirely within my grasp, I knew that what had happened then could happen again and I knew that those perpetrators were not 'them over there', they were also me.

Through my research I was discovering these 'ordinary' people, but I was also discovering the extraordinary. In 2006, Marc Rothemund's film *Sophie Scholl*[40] was nominated for the Best Foreign Film category in the Academy Awards. The subject of the film, Sophie Scholl, belonged to the White Rose, a student resistance movement in Germany founded by her older brother, Hans. The aim of the White Rose was to rouse thinking people to take part in passive resistance against the Nazi dictatorship. They did this by posting hundreds of leaflets all over Germany. These leaflets contained stringent analyses of the bankruptcy of Nazi ideology and a contrasting affirmation of the highest human values. They hoped that their words would give courage to those who disagreed with the system and awaken the conscience of those in its thrall. They hoped to foster a grassroots movement of resistance. The film focuses on Sophie's last six days, from the opening scene where she is preparing and distributing leaflets to the students in Munich University, to her capture, interrogation, trial and subsequent execution on 22 February 1943.

In 1947 Sophie's sister, Inge, published a book about the White Rose[41]. There she tells the story of herself, Sophie and her brother Hans in the 1930s. At first, they were seduced by the ideals of the Hitler Youth. They enjoyed belonging to a group, walking in the country and singing around the camp fire. They felt united, that they had found something worth living for: the youth movement became their *raison d'être*. Gradually, they began to have questions. Hans Scholl described the moment when, attending a rally as a flag bearer, he was berated for bringing his own personalised standard to the march. He glimpsed that the true nature of Nazism undermined the essential nature of the individual. He realised that he was expected to conform and lose sight of his essential self. As he shared his doubts with his sisters, other events confirmed their new perspective. A teacher they knew and respected was forced to stand whilst his pupils spat on him. He then disappeared. When the children asked why, his mother told them that he had gone to a concentration camp because he wouldn't join the Party. Everywhere they looked they saw horizons being narrowed as whole areas of music, literature and art were excluded and banned. Furthermore, no one could explain why the Jews were treated so badly. No longer able to identify with this poisonous ideology, Hans and his sisters found their initial feeling of joy and fellowship fading and being replaced by depression.

This depression was the beginning of their journey. They had entered the realm of negative capability, where they had lost their old certainties and not yet found their new standpoint and their new community. They had given their hearts to the youth movement and been bitterly disappointed.

Disappointment is a moment of trial. It can lead to bitterness and cynicism and a decision never to trust idealism again, or it can lead to a maturing and strengthening of idealism. To begin with, the Scholls were disillusioned. Then they began to read, think and talk, researching other examples from history that illuminated what was happening in their own lives. They studied how people had acted in past situations of oppression, and they learned from them. They were inspired by the Expressionist painters, by contemporary theology and political activism. When they finally decided to act they had a concrete goal, namely to inaugurate a movement of passive resistance in the heart of the Nazi state. They took these terrible risks because they believed that to be silent was to be complicit in this awful tyranny, and their conscience would not allow that. To know the truth and to do nothing was far more fearful a prospect than not acting.

When Sophie, Hans and their friend Christoph Probst were executed for high treason they were respectively twenty-one, twenty-four and twenty-three years old. Christoph was the father of three children. As part of the terror tactics of the state, they were guillotined. They were all students at the University of Munich. During their trial, Sophie accused the assembled courtroom of not having the courage to face the truth of Germany's imminent defeat, and defended their actions in resisting the system saying, "Someone had to make a start."

Later, Sophie's cellmate told her family about Sophie's last morning. She said that Sophie had had a dream in which she carried a child up a steep path to be baptised. As Sophie walked, the ground opened into a deep abyss, and she only just managed to place the child safely on the further side before she was swallowed up. Sophie was reassured by the dream, telling her cellmate that though they were going to die, their great idea would survive. Although they appeared helpless before the full wrath of the Nazi state they are now known all over the world as symbols of what is possible in the fight against tyranny.

Traudl Junge, Hitler's secretary, was a contemporary of the Scholl children. Before she died, she agreed to be interviewed, and the interview was made into a film called *Blind Spot*[42]. At the beginning of the interview, she appears to have nothing of great depth to say about what she witnessed, describing herself as too young and stupid to be aware of the atrocities carried out in the name of Nazism.

During the interview she takes a break and goes for a walk in the streets of Munich. This walk changes her. As she walks she comes across the monument to Sophie on the street in Munich. Looking at it and reading the text, she realises that she and Sophie were the same age. She then admits to herself, and to the camera, that hiding behind her youth when talking about her past had been a lie. She acknowledges that, if she had chosen, she, like Sophie, would have known what was going on ... instead, she had chosen to blot it out.

Sophie Scholl was executed on the 22nd of February, which happens to be my birthday. I have a picture of her and her brother on the wall in my study. It took me years to be able to put them up and, even now, they are slightly hidden behind a door. Their intelligence, their clarity, their conviction that they must not collude with injustice, and their absolute equanimity in the face of their daunting death, is so remarkable and so beyond my reach I can only look at their pictures now and then. Nevertheless I have put them up to remind me that human beings are capable of such deeds too. Stangl ignored his conscience and hid his decisions from his employer and his wife. Höss hated the violence in Dachau but denied and hid his softheartedness, choosing instead to harden himself lest he be despised for his vulnerability. Their failure to face themselves made them so lacking in selfhood that they could be persuaded to do things which stole their humanity, and destroyed the lives of millions.

In contrast, the Scholls were able to admit doubt in their youthful ideals, thereby starting the process of their awakening to selfhood. By losing their certainties and falling into uncertainty, they became depressed. They stayed with the consequences of their feelings and tried to find ways to understand and respond to their newly-emerging truths. From the moment they allowed their doubts space, they began a journey from 'group think' to individualisation, and from there to the freedom to act out of their true values.

Chapter 16
Social Sculpture: The Self as a Work of Art

In the introduction to this book I described making a project called *The Search for the Deep Self*. The work is made up of a circle of large banners, each of which shows the countenance of a person. Under their image is the story of one of their moments of becoming. You can see some of their stories in the appendix on page 139. It is not a static work. I use it to work with themes of self and becoming all over the world. Furthermore, as more and more people offer me their experiences, it continues to grow in compass. For me it will not be finished until it contains the story of every person in the world. It is a celebration of exactly this capacity to find out who we really are. I made it because I wanted to make visible this fear of self, and to encourage us to dare to embrace the joy of living out of our deepest values. The effect of doing this or not, both on an individual and a community, is profound, as the stories of Stangl or the White Rose illustrate.

My mother's fear of being seen in all her vulnerability, and her fear of her own creativity, were my teachers here. I knew that in order to make this work I had to find a way to make art which invited people to explore this sensitive subject without making them feel compelled, frightened or judged.

I undertook the project in the tradition of Joseph Beuys, the founder of Social Sculpture, as part of a Masters degree which I started in 2007. The theories and practice of Social Sculpture were profoundly important for me. They gave me a framework for my art, in that Social Sculpture widens the remit of art to include our inner lives, our capacity to respond and feel, and our capacity to work together for transformation. This inclusion of the whole person was essential for the exploration of my themes.

Beuys and his collaborators explored and discovered different strategies which made it possible, in the words of the poet Adrienne Rich, to 'invent more merciful instruments, to touch the wound beyond the wound.'[43] In other words: to make art which has the capacity to face what is painful in the spirit of healing.

Beuys began to work in this way in the aftermath of the Second World War. The cultural tendency he experienced in post-war Germany, to numb out and anaesthetise difficult feelings, to ignore and deny difficult events or memories meant that it was essential for him as an artist to find a way to approach the wounds of his culture in the spirit of both power and love. He knew it was important to be aware of sensitivities but also to be aware of the need for transformation. He created forms and actions where people were inspired to respond and feel, in other words to experience an enlivening of being as opposed to fearfully seeking numbness. Shelley Sacks, Beuys' pupil, calls this 'ethical aesthetics' because to be warmed and invited to respond can move us on from response to responsibility. In other words we are not only allowing the pain a space, we are also finding a way to respond to it, to transform it. This new aesthetic can become the antidote to the anaesthetic, the numbing out of so much of contemporary culture. This too resonated with my own agenda.

I had continued to carry the postcard of Beuys' work *Show Your Wound* around with me long after I left Germany. Producing my artwork for the Masters gave me a formal place for my intensity, thereby freeing me from the anxiety of not knowing how I could live in the world with my questions. I could 'be' intense, and show my wound, while at the same time turning that wound into an opportunity for others to find their potential. Beuys famously said that 'everyone is an artist'. Insofar as each one of us possesses an imagination, each one of us has the capacity to re-imagine, to re-mould or re-form the world. My interest in the realisation of self and our consequent capacity to realise our potential resonated profoundly with Beuys' assertion. Each one of us is an artist, and one's self and one's life has the possibility to be a work of art as well.

Thornton Wilder says, 'An artist is one who knows he is failing at living and feeds his remorse by making something fair.'[44] My work is my 'something fair', my struggle to find meaning and to not give in to incomprehension. Being able to explore, through my life and art, the questions my biography threw up has completely changed the way I see my early years. A mother is not simply a mother through the possession of that name. My mother was a struggling person. I do not blame her for anything that happened. I was someone she wrestled with as she wrestled with herself. I believe this was a fruitful struggle because through both of our efforts it became the means by which we both found ourselves.

● ● ● ● ● ● ●

Joseph Beuys was not the only artist to see the connection between the individual and the art they make. He was part of a wider tradition. The American poet and thinker Henry Thoreau said, 'I require of every writer first and last, a simple and sincere account of his own life, and not merely what he or she has heard of other men's lives.'[45] His countryman, Thornton Wilder, writing a hundred years later, said that if he had been brave enough he would never have invented characters for his novels but would have begun them all with the word 'I'.

In the past, history was about those at the top of the hierarchy. Ordinary people were mostly missing from the story. It was as recently as the First World War that memorials first began to name the hitherto anonymous foot soldiers that had died in battle. Our individual story has begun to count, to have significance.

This development can also be traced in the visual arts. Towards the end of the nineteenth century, the French Impressionists began to paint in a completely new way. They experienced the culture of their day as bankrupt. The old sources of inspiration – classical antiquity and established religion – had dried up. This gave birth to a revolution in painting. Turning away from conventional subjects, they chose instead to paint everyday life and ordinary people. They turned their gaze upon this previously unrecognised world, and in painting it they flooded their canvases with light. The laboratory where they searched for their new truth about humanity was the everyday world and ourselves. They were saying to their subjects, 'You and your deeds are no longer in the background of life's drama, you are centre stage.'

Another group of painters, the Post-Impressionists, then built on what they had achieved. A painting that embodies this new consciousness more than any other is *The Sower* by Vincent Van Gogh. This painting shows us what kind of human being was to be born out of that new laboratory of life, and what new responsibilities would be asked of us with our newly-found significance. In Van Gogh's own words: 'I want to paint men and women with something of the eternal which the halo used to symbolise, and which we seek to convey by the actual radiance and vibration of the colouring.'[46] Van Gogh paints the sower walking along a furrow. In his left hand he holds a pouch of seeds close to his heart. With his right hand he scatters the seeds onto the earth. He stands directly in front of the rising sun so that his head seems to be surrounded by a huge nimbus. He is lit up as if he were divine, no longer invisible, but the hero of a contemporary myth.

In the past, the heroes of the myths were special people, descended from the gods. When Van Gogh painted the sower, he did not paint the 'eternal' bestowed on special people as a birthright by a distant deity. Instead he is saying, at the hand of the sower: we are all special people and this quality of eternity or selfhood is possible for us all through the fruit of our own efforts.

The outer sun shining so radiantly around his head reflects the sun of his true self. To have achieved that radiant selfhood he has worked on his life, gaining knowledge and insight which, like seeds, he can now offer to future generations. It is this quality of the hero that we have also seen in the lives of the young people of the White Rose.

The history of art shows the changing role of the artist. In the myth of the good life, freedom and happiness are reduced to the lowest common denominator and the artist's role is to be just another producer of objects of consumption, admired only for the ability to command high prices. It is often the unbeguiled artists and thinkers in society who try to tell another story.

Just before the First World War, Wassily Kandinsky, Franz Marc and others formed a group called the 'Blue Rider'. They resolved to make and exhibit work that ran contrary to what they saw as the prevailing materialism of their time. In Franz Marc's words:

> To create forms means to live. Are not children who create directly from the secrets of their own emotions more creative than the imitators of Greek form? Are not the savage artists who have their own form stronger than the forms of thunder? We went with a divining rod through the art of the past and the art of the present. We showed only art which lives untouched by the constraints of convention. Our devoted care was extended to all artistic expression that was born of itself, lives on its own merit and does not walk on the crutches of custom. Whenever we have seen a crevice in the crust of convention we have called attention to it because we have hoped for a force underneath which will someday come to life.[47]

The artists of the Blue Rider showed the work of children, those who were called mad, and those artists deemed to be primitive. They were concerned not with beauty or good taste; they were concerned with authenticity, with truth, and with the individual's capacity to find his or her voice.

The Blue Rider was broken up by the outbreak of the First World War. As a Russian, Kandinsky had to leave Germany. After the war he returned and played a role in the founding of the Bauhaus, an artistic community which was formed in the spirit of the communities that grew up around the building of the great medieval cathedrals. Rather than building a house of God, the Bauhaus artists wanted to create the forms needed by the contemporary world and the contemporary human being.

Hitler's rise to power was to see that endeavour destroyed as well. In 1937, Goebbels organised an exhibition of so-called degenerate or anti-German art in Munich, which later toured throughout Germany. Many of the artists once connected with the Blue Rider, and many of those responsible for the Bauhaus, were included in this exhibition. It is said that the curator would have liked to have chained the artists beside their paintings so that they could be spat on. The capacity of artists to find their voice and work out their true self was exactly what the Nazis hated.

During the period of the Blue Rider, Kandinsky wrote a book called *Concerning the Spiritual in Art*[48], in which he outlines his ideas about art and the role of the artist. He believed that the artist's gifts bring responsibilities: they are asked to use their sensitivity to sense and bring to light the wounds of their time. Their work, born out of concern, then becomes a kind of medicine, an antidote to these wounds. Kandinsky was following in the footsteps of Friedrich Schiller, who said of the role of the artist, 'Live with your century but do not be its creature. Work for your contemporaries, but create what they need, not what they praise.'[49]

Perhaps the most visible wound of our time is the wound we have inflicted on the earth. Our feeling of entitlement to consume all we desire and our exploitation of nature cries out for our attention. Author and ecologist Alastair McIntosh says, 'I realise[d] that I have little optimism for the ability of our society to deal with climate change in terms of conventional political, economic and technological ideas. This is because our society's capacity to have a rich authentic inner life has been historically eviscerated by the effects of hubris... I therefore see a huge role for the artist in every sense of the word in the transition process. We need to see prophetic art – including poetry, music activism, you name it – stuff that sidesteps all the wackiness of narcissistic indulgence that often passes as art, and gets right to the one true function of the artist – to point towards the soul.'[50]

Chapter 17
Final Pieces Fall into Place

Victor E Frankl was a therapist working in Vienna at the same time as Adler and Freud. Just before the Nazi takeover of Austria he wrote the first draft of a book, which was later to become famous under the title *Man's Search for Meaning*[51]. He and his wife were transported to Auschwitz in 1944. As soon as they arrived, they were separated. She died in the gas chambers that same day. He was taken to the shower block where prisoners were shaved, tattooed and given their prison uniforms. Against the odds, he had managed to keep his manuscript with him. As he was shaved and tattooed he asked a fellow prisoner to help him to find a place to hide it. The prisoner pointed to the smoking chimneys of the crematoria. He told him what was happening in that terrible place. He told him his wife was dead and that he should forget his book. In the face of tragedy and almost certain death, Frankl decided that if he couldn't save his manuscript (which he was indeed unable to do), he would have to live it instead.

Man's Search for Meaning, which Frankl rewrote after he was released from Auschwitz and had published in Vienna in 1946, describes his therapeutic method, which he called Logotherapy. He summarised the essence of Logotherapy as follows:

As each situation in life represents a challenge to us, and presents us with a problem to solve, the question of the meaning of life may actually be reversed. Ultimately we should not ask what the meaning of our life is, but rather we should recognise it is we who are being asked. In a word each individual ... can only respond by being responsible. Thus Logotherapy sees responsibleness as the very essence of human existence. [52]

For Frankl, our struggles were opportunities to become inwardly free. Freedom does not come through perfect outer circumstances but through our capacity to respond creatively in whatever circumstance we find ourselves. Van Gogh's Sower is an image of the hero of the modern myth, becoming himself by overcoming his challenges, bearing his eternal nature as the fruit of his own struggles. Frankl's life is a confirmation of that prophetic work, but also a confirmation of what is possible for us all.

When I lived in Germany a friend came to visit me. She was on her way back from a trip to Romania, where she had been shocked to see real poverty: feral children living on the street. There was no infrastructure, none of the services that we take for granted, and this was in the heart of Europe! At the time, I was living in an exquisite villa on a hill overlooking Stuttgart. Our garden flat had beautiful wooden floors and French windows opening on to a terrace. Just outside my door there was a postbox. Every week a man with a truck would stop in my street and open up an organic shop from his van. Ten minutes from the flat was an internationally acclaimed art gallery, a market filled with produce from Italy, and a theatre and concert hall. We had health insurance; I had a studio; we could board a train and visit Italy. We lived in such luxury compared to so much of the world.

For me, this contrast in living conditions was a conscience call; if I had been freed from the basic fight for existence it was important not to waste the opportunities life gave me. I reinforced my commitment to engage with my own story and my own life, to embrace my intensity and go on my own hero's journey. The stories of Stangl, Höss and Frankl happened during the Second World War in a time of tyranny. It was very clear, then, to see the line between good and evil. Is that line as clear for us? If we don't live under tyranny, can we relax and be sure that our unexamined lives can never cause deep harm? The next story that I came across helped me in developing and working with this question.

· · · · · · ·

I first read Bill Wiseman's story in an article in the Saturday Guardian magazine[53]. Wiseman was the American politician who introduced the lethal injection as a supposedly humane form of execution. In 1972, capital punishment in the US had effectively been embargoed by the Supreme Court's decision that, as it was then being applied, it constituted 'cruel and unusual punishment', and as such was a violation of the Constitution. Since the lethal injection was deemed to be 'humane', the constitutional challenge to the death penalty was lifted, and lethal injection became the most commonly used means of execution in the USA from the late 1970s.

Wiseman described his reasons for getting involved with politics in the following way:

> I thought I could be very competent as a legislator. Secondly I liked the idea that it gave me an identity. I have always lived in the shadow of my father, and it would be a chance to take all these ideas I have on ethics and moral behaviour and do something about them.

He followed his political ambitions and became a respected member of the Oklahoma legislature. During his time in office, the question of capital punishment came up for debate. At that time, no politician could succeed without supporting the death penalty.

Wiseman had become so dependent on his role, and on the status it offered him, that he found himself prepared to do anything to stay in power. This included voting for the death penalty, which was something that he categorically did not believe in.

Feeling guilty for having voted for the death penalty, Wiseman tried to assuage his conscience. He called the State Medical Examiner, Jay Rayner, to ask him whether he knew of a more humane way of conducting executions. As it happened, Rayner did. He dictated the recipe to Bill Wiseman, who had no medical training and no way of assessing whether this was a good solution or not. Wiseman drafted a statute containing the recipe for 'an ultra-short-acting barbiturate in combination with a chemical paralytic.'[54]

To Wiseman's amazement, the statute was adopted. He was invited to talk on television; he was featured in national magazines. He became a celebrity: the man who had made the death penalty compassionate.

Campaigners against the death penalty warned him many times that if 'the stench and pain' were removed from execution, if it appeared painless and easy, far more people would be executed than previously. He took no notice of their warnings. Not only did he want to keep his job, his high profile in the media had given him an even more intoxicating sense of being 'someone'. He said of himself at this time, 'I must admit, staying in office became my top priority. I had an identity, a mission, and all kinds of recognition. Anything that would threaten that would strike a dark hidden terror.'[55] His wish to be 'someone' had become more important than what kind of person that 'someone' was.

In the interview in The Guardian, Bill Wiseman said that only after eight hundred people had been executed using the lethal injection did he come to his senses. He recanted from his position and joined the campaign to abolish the death penalty. He lost his seat on the Oklahoma legislature because he took this stand. He said that he would always remain aware of the part he had played in each and every execution. He said of his reasons for recanting his position:

> *I am opposed to the death penalty because of what it does to us – not what it does to the person who dies – how it changes us and identifies us as a society when we make a corporate decision to take a life. All that stuff about how it is incompetent or unfair, that's all very interesting but it is not the point. The point is we must not do this because it eats away at our soul.*[56]

Bill Wiseman's story shook me to my core. In the richest democracy in the world, the land of the free, he had lost his humanity. His wish to be someone, to flee what he called 'his dark hidden terror', was so overpowering that he had been willing to ignore his conscience. In the words of Becker, it is 'normal average men who lay waste to the world in order to flee from themselves.'[57] When I set Wiseman's story next to that of Victor Frankl, who was able to remain free and human even in the concentration camps of Nazi Germany, I understood that it was not the regime or the circumstances that were the issue, it was us. We were the deciding factor in who we became, and what effects we had on the world.

I cannot demand that anyone else change, but I can try to change myself. By taking seriously the work of my own self-becoming and my own capacity to live creatively or not, I am choosing to build the inner muscles, the inner character that may be needed in more demanding times. By demanding this of myself, it is possible to live a more privileged existence in full awareness of my responsibilities as well as my advantages. It is for this reason that I chose to work not only as a painter but also as a Social Sculptor, creating work that attempts to contribute to our capacity to heal rather than harm.

Chapter 18
Widening Circles

Beuys was very concerned with our capacity to be free and our capacity to join together to build a better world, an ecological society. I see from my experience in many settings that it doesn't matter how beautiful our ideas are, they can only be put into practice if we become individuals. When, as individuals, we work with others out of an ever-deepening inner truth that is neither conformity nor dogma, we cease to live in abstractions. Instead of being disconnected we connect and we begin to feel responsible for the suffering of the world. Out of this empathy we choose to do good because we have understood why it matters that we do it. We are not the puppets of our fears and anxieties, nor are we the instruments of false ideologies. We are free human beings.

To work like this takes time, energy and concern. It is a never-ending process. Joseph Beuys called it a state of permanent conference. It is only possible if we care enough to respond. Responding makes us responsible. If we begin to work in this way, we reconnect with the real story of freedom and happiness which can be found deep beneath the surface noise of the story of the good life.

In the year 2000, Paul Ray and his wife, Sherry Anderson, published a book called *Cultural Creatives*[58]. The result of many years of research, it demonstrates through stories and interviews that there are ever growing sub-cultures in American society. The authors have since repeated their research in Europe where they have found the same phenomenon. Groups of people, disillusioned by mainstream culture, have turned inward to examine their lives, and then turned back to the world with new values.

Cultural creatives come from every walk of life. Their concerns are wide and include authenticity, idealism, activism, globalism and ecology, women's rights, altruism, self-actualisation and spirituality. At the time of writing their book, Paul Ray and Sherry Anderson estimated that at least fifty million Americans belong to such groups. They wrote their book to ensure that individuals with these new, non-mainstream values would have a name. By having an identity they would then have the capacity to connect with each other and use the power of their numbers to influence policy and change that mainstream culture that had left them so disillusioned.

In 2005 Peter Senge, C Otto Scharmer, Joseph Jaworski and Betty Sue Flowers published a book called *Presence: An Exploration of Profound Change in People, Organisations and Society*[59]. They are part of an organisation called the Society for Organizational Learning, a non-profit, international membership organisation that connects researchers, organisations and consultants in over thirty countries to build knowledge for systematic change. One of the main theories that Scharmer explored in the book was called *Theory U*. As a young boy, Scharmer was called home from school because the family farm had burned to the ground. His family had lived there for two hundred and fifty years. Coming face to face with the total destruction of his family home, his first experience was one of attachment to all the things destroyed in the fire, and grief that everything was gone. He went on:

> But no – I realized not everything was gone: there was a tiny element of myself that wasn't gone with the fire. I was still there watching ... the seer. I suddenly realized there was another whole dimension of myself that I hadn't been aware

of ... At that moment time slowed down to complete stillness and I felt drawn in a direction above my physical body ... I felt my mind expanding to a moment of unparalleled clarity of awareness. I realized I was not the person I thought I was. My real self was not attached to the tons of stuff now smouldering in the ruins. I suddenly knew that I, my true Self, was still alive, more awake, more acutely present than ever before ... At that moment with everything gone, I suddenly felt released to encounter that part of myself, the part that drew me into the future ... into my future ... and into a world that I might bring into reality in my life. [60]

He went on to research what he had experienced spontaneously in his youth, and developed a way to cultivate that experience consciously, thus empowering us to meet crises or conflict with new organs of perception, with capacities beyond the rational mind.

To develop these capacities, Scharmer says that you have to go deep down into experience, to the bottom of the U, before coming out again. The self that one connects with at the bottom of the U is not our ordinary, everyday self. Scharmer describes this as the Self with a capital 'S', our highest future possibility.

This is the self I have tried to make visible in my work. It has a paradoxical quality. One can see it most starkly in people like Sophie Scholl or Victor Frankl. They are not selfish, nor are they lacking a self, or self-less. Rather they are a strong self. When they achieve their full selfhood, they choose to serve. They may be held in captivity by the powers of the world but they have found a place of freedom in themselves that nothing can violate. In the words of Joseph Jaworski, 'you discover who you really are as a steward for what is needed in the world.'[61] In order to do this work, people are willing to, and often need to, give up money and status. A sense of meaning is more important than these outer rewards. The freedom to do what we like, and consume what we want, does not truly nourish us. People long for a deeper sense of freedom and happiness.

In 1991 Suzi Gablik, the artist, teacher and writer, published a book called *The Re-enchantment of Art*. She hoped for the emergence of a new kind of art that would foster what she too believed was an emerging change in thinking and being. She says:

> *If a new kind of self – the ecological self – does truly emerge in our culture, it will challenge the assumption that human beings are basically selfish and motivated entirely by economics. Obviously what is being suggested involves a revolution in consciousness as far reaching as the emergence of individualism itself was during the Renaissance.*[62]

This new kind of self, this new hero, is beginning to appear. The heroes of old had to face many tests in order to achieve their goals. Before Heracles began his labours he first had to choose which kind of life he would live. This was his first test. It begins when he meets two women who each offer to guide him on his way. The first one says to him:

> *Dear Heracles, I see that you have reached the age when you must choose what kind of life yours is to be. So I have come to urge you to take me as your friend and let me guide you on your way. I promise that if you do I will lead you by the easiest and most delightful paths. You shall taste every pleasure, and no troubles or toils shall come near you. Your life shall be passed in the pursuit and enjoyment of pleasant things, with no labour of body or mind, except to please yourself without any thought for the cares of others.*

After she has finished speaking Heracles asks her name. Unable to look him in the eye, she answers:

Heracles, those who love me call me Happiness, but my enemies, it is true, have another name which I do not care to mention.

The second woman then speaks to him. She says:

I too, noble Heracles, am come to offer you a way of life. Follow me, and you will do great deeds and leave a name which will never be forgotten. But you cannot win what is glorious and excellent in the world without care and labour. The gods give no real good, no true happiness to men on earth on any other terms. If you would bring happiness to others and be remembered in Greece, you must strive for the service of Greece – as you well may with your strength and your skill, if you do but use them rightly. As for my companion, who is called Vice and Folly and other such names, do not be misled by her. There is no pleasure and no happiness like those which you earn by strife and labour and with the sweat of your brow.

Vice tempts Hercules further. She says:

Do not believe this foolish girl, who is called Virtue! My way to happiness is short and pleasant; hers is hard, and long, and the end is doubtful.

The second woman then turns to Heracles and says:

Choose which of us you will follow. Her path leads through easy, worthless pleasures that grow stale and horrible and yet are craved after more and more. But follow me through toil and suffering to the great heritage which Zeus has planned for you.[63]

The same choice faces us today. Unlike Heracles, few of us have a wise teacher to instruct us what to do. Yet, like him, we must decide. The first choice sounds very like the choice offered by the myth of the good life. The second is much harder.

My work, and indeed the practice of Social Sculpture, is all about fostering this newly-emerging self, but in the end it is not beautiful ideas that make such a self possible. Whether ideas bear fruit will always depend on the alchemy between the world and the individual; it is my choice how I will respond to my challenges. We may look to parents, mentors and teachers, but often they are as lost as us. Our training is our life, our 'vale of soul making'. This is a never-ending process. Although we may achieve selfhood in one situation, that will not be the end of the struggle. Becoming a self is a process; it needs to happen not once but over and over. We will repeatedly meet the beguiling myth of the good life and have to choose whether to lose ourselves to it or not. If we choose not to, we can join this ever-growing constituency described by the writers of Cultural Creatives; those who have turned inward in order to find other values by which to live.

· · · · · · ·

In the past, artists transformed substance to make objects. Now a new art has been born in which we are the substance. What we can make of that substance is our deep self. The capacity to become our best self draws us out of the shadows onto the stage. We are asked to find our part and play it. The skill that we need to transform ourselves into that deeper self is the capacity to die and become. As we die, we have to learn how to endure the awful anxiety and emptiness that greets us as we let go of what we were, and wait to hear what we can be. Even if we achieve this once, twice or many more times, still there is no rest. The process needs to happen time and time again and each time we meet the challenge anew it still remains heart-wrenchingly difficult and often we will stumble.

Sometimes it is possible to find friends along the way. Like us, they are challenged. Each of us has one thing in common. We will fail time and time again. Our friendship is not born out of all our glories. It is born out of our capacity to admit our failures and to try again. Trust is born not from our being perfect but rather when we can acknowledge our mistakes and grow from them. Friends who share this trust become helpers on our way. They can also become colleagues who join together to do the work of transformation.

Our security as individuals and as groups cannot come from the absence of pain or catastrophe, nor can it come from adamantine certainty which makes us simplify life into dead dogmas and fanaticism, and removes us from the flow of process. Kierkegaard said, 'He who cannot reveal himself cannot love.'[64] To show one's wound is to agree to be visible, to own one's vulnerability and thereby connect with our fellow human beings who are all equally vulnerable.

In the past, we have looked up into the sky searching for God. We have given our power away to outer authorities and we have done what they told us to do. Now we have the capacity to be our own authority and to form circles and communities willing to search for our own solutions. Now, if we want to experience the divine, we do not need to search the sky. The divine, the eternal painted by Van Gogh, is not far away; it is in the countenance of those friends and colleagues who are strong, not through their invincibility but through their capacity to give themselves to the never-ending process of learning with all the vulnerability that that entails.

Viktor Frankl said:

> *Do not aim at success – the more you aim at it and make it your target, the more you will miss it. For success, like happiness, cannot be pursued; it must ensue, and it only does so as the*

unintended side effect of one's personal dedication to a cause greater than oneself, or as the product of one's surrender to a person other than oneself ... I want you to listen to your conscience and what it commands you and go away and carry it out to the best of your knowledge. Then you will live to see in the long run – and I say the long run – success will follow you precisely because you had forgotten to think about it.[65]

This is what it means to be free; this is what it means to be happy; this is what it means to dig below the surface myth of the good life to the deeper story that is asking us to be co-creators of an ever richer reality.

Acknowledgements

Thank you to my first editor Rob Porteous for two years' hard work.

Thank you Sarah Bird who despite illness worked on the final version and made it all fall into place.

Thank you to my husband Tom who always helps with all my work as if it was as important as his own.

And thank you as well:

To Richard Heys who designed the cover.

To Chris Seeley who helped bring about the publication.

To Jane Chase who freely gave her work as a photographer for the project.

To Harriet Harris who first affirmed what I had written and gave me the courage to take it further.

To Jean Flyn who has supported my work in terms of belief and practical contributions.

To Rosie Phillpot and Tom Hart-Shea for their warmth and support in getting my work into the world.

To every person who so generously gave me their stories for The Search for the Deep Self Project.

To Adam Kahane who gave me an essential clue with his work with love and power.

To the students of Leith School of Art who encouraged me to write down my lectures.

To Mike Chase whose artistic collaboration with me and others was so productive.

To my community in Stourbridge for their constant encouragement and interest.

To Kerstin Cuming who helped me take my work around

Germany and Great Britain.

To Christiaan Franken for practical help in making my project possible.

To Anne Byrne for love and practical help in every aspect of my work.

To Michael Kienzler who helped me understand Goethe's poem.

To Christine Deacon who first introduced me to Joseph Beuys and gave me the image of Beuys' work, *Show Your Wound*.

To Maria Mountain and Annette Gordon for proofreading, and to Denis Kennedy for copy-editing.

Appendix: The Search for the Deep Self

This book begins with a description of the moment when I conceived the idea for my project, 'The Search for the Deep Self'.

This project documents descriptions of moments when people came into connection with their deepest being. These can be moments of hardship and challenge, or moments of clarity and oneness with our deepest purpose. The stories are presented with a portrait photograph of the person above each one.

I have printed the stories on a set of banners which are set out in a circle, within which a large group of people may gather to work with me. The project can be seen on the internet at www.becomingaself.org. There is also a kit, consisting of a box of cards, each with one story. These cards can then be set up anywhere: in a kitchen, on a train or in any setting in which a group of people wish to explore their relationship to their deepest purpose.

This appendix shows eight of the many stories that I have collected. I have chosen them in order to give some idea of the quality and variety of the stories and each person's unique challenges.

If you wish to explore more, please look at the website: www.becomingaself.org. If you would like to share a story, to work with the project with a group, or to get hold of a kit, please contact me at info@becomingaself.org

David Bomberg

David Bomberg was a working-class Jewish boy who made it to art school and believed in the ideals of modernism. He was deeply influenced by the dream of a future in which machines would free us from having to work. Called up to fight in the trenches of the First World War, he witnessed unbearable carnage and got himself discharged by shooting himself in the foot. In doing this he risked being shot for cowardice. After his experiences in the trenches he suffered a severe depression. His whole view of life, his standpoint, had been called into question by the reality of war. He felt a deep need not to be abstract, but to find what one lived for out of real experience, not theories. He then rejected all the ideas of modernism, feeling that he had seen the consequences of modern technology untamed by human values, first hand. He said:

> We have no need to dwell on the material significance of man's achievements...but with the approach of scientific mechanization and the submerging of individuals we have urgent need of the affirmation of his spiritual significance and his individuality.

By speaking as he did and painting in a new way, he lost credibility in the fashionable art world and lived in great poverty. Despite treading this lonely path he never compromised, as he believed that art without integrity was nothing. Towards the end of his life, he taught in the Borough Polytechnic in London and became known as the greatest teacher of the age by his students. He only received real recognition after his death.

Gideon Byamugisha

Gideon is a minister in the Anglican Church of Uganda. In 1992 he became the first African religious leader to announce publicly that he was HIV-positive.

Gideon was about to come to Britain to study with his wife when she suddenly became seriously ill and died. Gideon's sister-in-law found out that his wife had died of AIDS, but she kept the information to herself. Gideon was completing his studies; she feared that the bereavement and the potential implications of an AIDS diagnosis would be too much to bear at that critical moment of his education. When he had finished his exams she told him what she knew and advised him to get an AIDS test. It took him three months to pluck up the courage to do this. He said what gave him the strength to go was that he realised that if he could survive the death of his beloved wife of twenty-five years, nothing could destroy him.

He received the results of his test from a counsellor, who looked at his priestly collar and said with a mocking voice, 'Man of God, what are you going to do now?' From that moment, Gideon entered a land that was foreign to him: the land of stigma.

To have an HIV-positive diagnosis in Uganda at that time meant that one had been cursed by God. The illness was connected to prostitution, homosexuals - so-called 'sexual deviants' - and long-distance lorry drivers who had many sexual partners. Gideon's career as a minister and lecturer in a theological college was over.

As he travelled home he had debated with himself.

He was devastated. He could choose to be silent and lead a double life. He knew however that that was not acceptable for a man of faith.

Spiritually he knew that he needed the support of fellow Christians to bear what was happening to him. They couldn't help him if he didn't tell them.

He knew as well that he would need the help of friends and family to get medicine and receive care.

He knew that silence would mean that he had no community. He resolved to trust in God and to be open instead of protecting himself from shame.

First he disclosed his situation to the principal of his college and his wife's sister. Then he told the college staff and his students and eventually his Bishop.

A person with AIDS needs a circle of support at work, in his church and in his family. That circle of support is open but at the same time it is confidential.

Gideon realised that there is another form of openness: to become completely publicly open. This is not something that everyone needs to do or even has the strength to do. It is a tough choice, which demands a lot of sacrifice. It is a calling.

The counsellor who handed him his results thrust Gideon into the world of stigma. This was also the first step on his journey towards his calling. Gideon discovered that he could use his position to uphold the dignity of those who were stigmatized everywhere in Africa. He is now able to feel gratitude towards the man who spoke to him as he did in his moment of supreme vulnerability. It was that experience which awoke him to the needs of his fellow human beings in a new way.

Gideon has since won the Niwano Peace Prize in recognition of his work in upholding the dignity and human rights of people living with AIDS.

Michael Chase

When I was fifteen years old, I was sent to a criminal juvenile institution for possessing drugs while being out of school and under age in South Africa.

After having been there for a term, I ran away while being escorted by a guard to a holiday camp. As I was being chased by station guards, I made my way to a nearby dual carriageway where I hid in a ditch. I thought I was safe and free. As I lay there, I began to feel that rather than being safe I was actually in an abyss, a place of abandonment and isolation both inwardly and outwardly. In that dark place I realized I had a choice to make: to stay there and keep running or to go back to my prison on my own terms. I chose to go back and I recommitted myself to the institution. From that moment I began to draw. I drew faces, faces with every possible expression, the myriad selves of my soul life, both creative and destructive. This was the beginning of my journey to my present work as a mask practitioner. I walked back to my prison in order to learn that freedom was an inner quality, and that it is not about doing what you like but doing what you really wish to do. I didn't want to wreck my body with drugs or risk my life on the edge and I needed to get hold of my own inner world, to be the director of my soul, rather than driven by it. It is this process that is now the central theme of my own work with masks.

Mark Chitty

I had a privileged upbringing. My stable family and expensive education had given me a can-do approach to life which had always seen me through any difficulties and challenges I had met.

In my late twenties, with a burgeoning career in London, a happy marriage and a demanding two year old son, my wife Ruth suddenly became seriously ill. At first I met this situation with my usual optimism. "Ah, she'll be back on her feet in no time," I would say to friends and family. And even as the weeks of pain and sickness turned into months of hospital visits and no clear prognosis, I continued to behave as if 'next week' Ruth would be better.

A cycle of endless work unfolded. My mother-in-law came up from Devon to look after my wife and son during the week. I took over in the evenings and weekends. The months passed. My life was gradually squeezed thinner and thinner.

Then one unremarkable evening, many months on, something happened. As usual, I came home from work, I plodded through the routine of putting my son to bed, I helped Ruth out, and I finally collapsed on the sofa with a beer, staring vacantly at the wall. But this evening I was struck by a new thought. I had been doing this for 8 months now. Ruth was still seriously ill. 'Next week' things were not going to be any better. Shit.

This realization prompted a fundamental shift in my thinking. For the first time in my life I couldn't fix a problem by doing. Ruth was ill. Nothing seemed to help. She might be ill for years. She may never even get better. So now what? How could I live with this new reality? Was there a way to stop fighting it and bend with it instead?

With this change, this facing of facts, this admitting defeat, there came an internal letting go of my rigid mantra that had always declared: 'This is who I am and this is how my life should be'. This shift suddenly opened up a whole new set of creative opportunities. My helplessness, when I finally acknowledged it, turned out not to be crushing and disempowering as I had expected. Instead it opened the door to a new roomful of inner resources I never knew existed: resources that could foster inner fluidity and help me to see myself not as a fixed point, an immutable pillar of rightness in a world gone wrong, but as a creature that could adapt and learn and grow and change its perceptions and responses to the world. I had found a whole new axis of movement in which to cultivate being alive.

Kerstin Cuming

Being afraid to hurt anyone
Being afraid to offend anyone
Being afraid to say the wrong thing
Being afraid to make any mistakes
Being afraid to move in the world
Being afraid to take up space
Being afraid to speak

For more than two decades I was desperately trying to change myself into someone else because I was told - and I believed - that I was not good enough the way I was.

I lost myself in the process and was becoming increasingly meek, heartbroken, empty, tired, invisible and silent.

NOOOOO.

A sound so unfamiliar, enormous, exasperated and raw erupted from my throat and escaped my lips.

It rose up from the deepest forgotten parts of my belly.

It had grown, taken shape and gathered strength during those many long years of desperation, loneliness, silence, fear and self-doubt.

A force so strong it shook every single cell of my body.

This single moment in time was my turning point.

I had found my voice.

It was the tenderest beginning of my becoming a self,

becoming my Self.

From that time onwards my journey is taking me one courageous step at a time on a soul-expanding, life-affirming and freeing new adventure into life.

Rosemary Merriman

For many years I lived in a state of despair, so that by the time I reached my late forties I had lost all hope that there was anything that could help me. I coped by trying to live my life as if I were normal, despite my overwhelming sense of gloom. Occasionally I would have dreams where I would experience a gleam of hope, only to wake and find that faint gleam had faded away. One day, as I hung around at home in this state of inner chaos, a leaflet came through the door. I picked it up. The leaflet had an image on it showing elderly people engaged in learning. There was a headline which said, 'Research reveals that old brains can grow new brain cells by learning new skills.' As I read the text I had the thought, 'If old people can grow new brain cells then perhaps I can.' I had always felt that the person who I truly was did not have the resources to transform my inner state. These words suggested I did. This was the moment that the hope that so eluded me when I woke from sleep began to take root in my waking life, and I slowly began to know recovery was possible for me.

Sir Martin Ryle

Sir Martin Ryle, the Astronomer Royal from 1972 to 1982, was a highly-acclaimed fellow of Trinity College Cambridge and the recipient of many awards from the establishment including the Nobel Prize for Physics. In the last ten years of his life he dedicated all his energy to attacking both nuclear power and the weapons industry it helped make possible. Many successful mainstream scientists considered the fact that he spent the last years of his life working in this field to be eccentric and a waste of Martin's skills. Despite seeing both his supporters and himself marginalized he continued to work to raise consciousness about these important issues. After he died these words were found scribbled among his papers:

Our world is one – yet evolution has now reached the stage where as a species we may die. We as scientists should be able to see this more clearly than most and we must use our influence to change the too limited aspirations of our governments. As scientists we must do all we can to prevent further misapplication of our work to provide weapons of war – instead we should strive to see how the vast resources now diverted towards the destruction of life are turned instead to the solution of the problems which both rich – but especially the poor – countries of the world now face.

Michael Rowan-Robinson, Reader in Astronomy at Queen Mary College, University of London, wrote (in a booklet called *Martin Ryle's Letter*) that Martin Ryle's example will not after all be remembered as quixotic, but rather a turning point in the responsibility of science and scientists.

Marcia Torres

Marcia is from Venezuela. She was twenty-eight when I heard her story. She came from a family where the adults were so vulnerable themselves that they couldn't be nurturing parents. Marcia worked in an ice-cream shop and loved mountain biking. Her only security was her work and her boyfriend Sandro. She told me that she and all her friends had no personal dreams. Instead they watched American soap operas all the time. They existed only to make enough money and to live through these make-believe worlds.

This period of her life came to an abrupt end when Sandro was killed in an accident.

No longer able to cope with her life in Venezuela, Marcia looked on the internet to find a place to work in Britain. She chose a community in Sussex that was inspired by the work of Rudolf Steiner, of whom Marcia had never heard. From there she found out about the existence of eurythmy – a form of movement inspired by Steiner. Although she did not have a penny to her name, nor any security, she applied to study eurythmy in a small school in the West Midlands in England. She has pursued this training ever since, working every spare hour to fund her existence.

Marcia attended an event where she saw some of these stories. Afterwards she came home with me and told me her story. She asked if it was possible to translate the stories into Spanish and to take the exhibition back to Venezuela. She said she herself had been caught in a kind of hypnosis that was only broken by the death of her boyfriend. This had been hard but it had meant that she had had the chance to find her own life and her own story. She wanted to show this work to her old friends in the hope that they too would respond to it, and that they could discover that their lives were significant and worth searching for.

Notes and References

1   Rilke, Rainer, *Duino Elegies*, trans J B Lieshman & S Spender, Chatto & Windus Ltd, 1981, p. 16

2   ibid

3   ibid, pp. 142, 143

4   Wordsworth, William, Ode: *Intimations of Immortality from Recollections of Early Childhood* cp http://www.bartleby.com/101/536.html

5   Rowling, J.K., *Harry Potter and the Philosopher's Stone*, Bloomsbury, 2015

6   Tolstoy, Leo, *Anna Karenina*, Penguin, 1972

7   Forster, E M, *Where Angels Fear to Tread*, Penguin, 1985, p 133

8   Wordsworth, William, cp http://www.bartleby.com/145ww317.html

9   Fromm, Erich, *To Have and To Be*, Continuum, 2008, p.31

10   Franklin, Miles, *My Brilliant Career*, CreateSpace Independent Publishing Platform, 2015

11   Franklin, Miles, *My Career Goes Bung*, CreateSpace Independent Publishing Platform, 2015

12   Leavis, F R, *The Great Tradition*, Penguin, 1983

13   Arcana, Judith, *Our Mothers' Daughters*, The Women's Press Ltd; Reprint edition, 1981

14   Estes, Clarissa Pinkola, *Women who run with Wolves*, Rider Classic Ed edition, 2008

15   Ibsen, Henrik, *Peer Gynt* trans. Christopher Fry and Johan Fillinger, Oxford University Press, 1989

16 Goethe, J W, *Blessed Longing*, trans. Stanton, Keith, Trafford Publishing, 2009, p. 66

17 Keats, John, *The Letters of John Keats*, ed. by H E Rollins, 2 vols, Cambridge: Cambridge University Press, 1958, pp.193-4

18 Conford, Philip (ed.), *The Personal World - John Macmurray on Self and Society,* Floris Books, 1996, p. 201

19 ibid, pp. 215-216

20 Brittain, Vera, *Testament of Youth*, Virago, 2014

21 Quoted in Borer, Alain and Schirmer, Lothar, *The Essential Joseph Beuys*, Thames and Hudson, 1997, p. 25

22 Rilke, Rainer-Maria, *Letters to a Young Poet*, W.W. Norton, 1962

23 See *Solving Tough Problems: An Open Way of Talking, Listening, and Creating New Realities*, 2007, *Power and Love: A Theory and Practice of Social Change*, 2010, *Transformative Scenario Planning: Working Together to Change the Future*, 2012

24 Quoted in Kahane, Adam, *Power and Love: A Theory and Practice of Social Change*, BK, 2010, p. 2

25 ibid, p. 8

26 Scott Peck was a psychiatrist who wrote several books about how to be a whole human being and about community. The two most famous are *The Road Less Travelled*, published in 1978, by Simon and Schuster, which explores the theme of human wholeness, and *The Different Drum: Community Making and Making Peace* which explores the challenges of making community. Also Simon and Schuster, 1987

27 Tutu, Desmond, *No Future Without Forgiveness*, Rider 1999, p 32

28 Dorfman, Ariel, *Death and the Maiden*, Nick Hern Books, 1996

29 Keller, Helen, *The Story of My Life*, Bantam, 1991

30   Quoted in Palmer, *Let Your Life Speak*, JosseyBass, 2000, p16

31   Rich, Adrienne, *On Lies, Secrets and Silences,* ,Virago, 1980, pp. 155-6

32   Keats, John, Section from John Keats's letter to his brother and sister-in-law, George and Georgiana Keats, written from 14 February to 3 May 1819; in *The Letters of John Keats*, 1814-1821, edited by Hyder Edward Rollins Harvard U.P., Cambridge, MA, 1958), pp. 100-104.

33   Harvey, Nicholas Peter, *The Morals of Jesus*, DLT, 1991, p. 43

34   Forster, ibid, p. 133

35   Uris, Leon, *Exodus*, Turtleback Books, 1983

36   Sereny, Gitta, *Into the Darkness*, Vintage, 1995

37   Ibid p 366

38   Hoess, Rudolf, *The Commandant*, Gerald Duckworth & Co Ltd, 2012

39   http://www.dailymail.co.uk/news/article-3105781/My beautiful-childhood-Daughter-Rudolph-Hoess-inspired trial-Bookkeeper-Auschwitz-talk-life-growing-concentration-camp-forgiven-Jewish-boss.html

40   Rothemund, Marc (directed), *Sophie Scholl*

41   Scholl, Inge, *The White Rose: Munich, 1942-1943*, Wesleyan, 1983

42   Heller, Andre (director), *Blind Spot - Hitler's Secretary*, Sony Pictures Home Entertainment, 2003

43   Rich, Adrienne, 'Natural Resources' in *The Dream of a Common Language*, Norton, 1978, p. 63

44   Wilder, Thornton, *The Collected Short Plays of Thornton Wilder, Vol. II*, Theater Communications Group, 1998, p. 4

45   Thoreau, Henry David, *Walden: Or, Life in the Woods*, Dover Thrift Editions, 1995, p. 2

46   Bernard, Bruce, *Vincent by Himself*, Macdonald and co Publishers, 1985, p.188.

47   *The Blaue Reiter Almanac*, Wassily Kandinsky and Franz

Marc (eds), Museum of Fine Arts, Boston, 2005, from the Foreword to the 2nd edition

48   Kandinsky, Wassily, *Concerning the Spiritual in Art*, trans. M. T. H. Sadler, Dover Publications, 1971

49   Schiller, J.C.F., *On the Aesthetic Education of Man*, trans. E.M. Wilkinson, L. A. Willoughby, Oxford University Press USA, 1983

50   McIntosh, Alastair, interview for the journal of the Ruskin Mill Educational Trust, spring 2008, p. 31

51   Frankl, Viktor, *Man's Search for Meaning*, Pocket Books (Simon & Schuster), 1984

52   ibid page 131

53   The Guardian (September 23, 2006)

54   ibid

55   ibid

56   ibid

57   Becker, quoted in Harvey (see note 33 above)

58   Anderson, Sherry Ruth, and Ray, Paul H., *Cultural Creatives*, Broadway Books, 2001

59   Senge, Peter, Scharmer, C. Otto and Jaworski, J, *Presence: Human Purpose and the Field of the Future*, Crown Business, 2008

60   ibid p. 81

61   ibid p. 91

62   Gablik, Suzi, *The Reenchantment of Art*, Thames and Hudson, 1995, p. 176

63   Green, Roger Lancelyn, *Tales of the Greek Heroes*, Puffin, 2009

64   Quoted in Flynn, Thomas, *Existentialism,* Sterling, 2006, p39

65   Frankl, ibid, p.17